CELEBRATING
EASTBOURNE

KEVIN GORDON

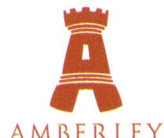

AMBERLEY

First published 2024

Amberley Publishing, The Hill, Stroud
Gloucestershire GL5 4EP

www.amberley-books.com

British Library Cataloguing in Publication Data.
A catalogue record for this book is available from the British Library.

ISBN 978 1 3981 0038 1 (print)
ISBN 978 1 3981 0039 8 (ebook)

Typesetting by SJmagic DESIGN SERVICES, India.
Printed in Great Britain.

Contents

Introduction

I love Eastbourne. I was born in the town, as were my ancestors, and I know they loved Eastbourne too. My great-grandfather Ebenezer Roberts wrote poems extolling the virtues of the town:

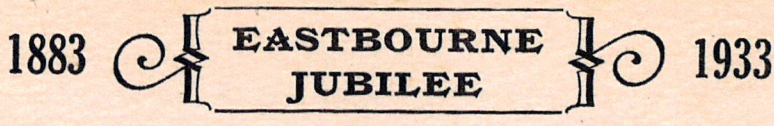

1883   EASTBOURNE JUBILEE   1933

Elegant spot of the Sunny South,
A mansion enclosed with hills round about;
Surrounded with beautiful foliage green,
To equal its splendour can never be seen—
Behold where you may it is pleasant and bright,
Of things that recruit the health and the sight;
Undone from the city you here can find rest,
Refreshed by the breezes that blow from the west:
New vigour obtained by a stroll near the sea—
Empress of the South let its name ever be.

E. ROBERTS.

I live in the heart of the 'Old Town' close to the massive parish church, and when I hear the church bells ringing across the town, I know it is the same sound that my ancestors heard.

Eastbourne is a town to be celebrated. It's location on the warm southern coast, protected by the rolling, whale-shaped South Downs, makes it an ideal place to live and the area has been occupied for millennia.

In this book I hope to celebrate Eastbourne through its varied history, unique places and remarkable people.

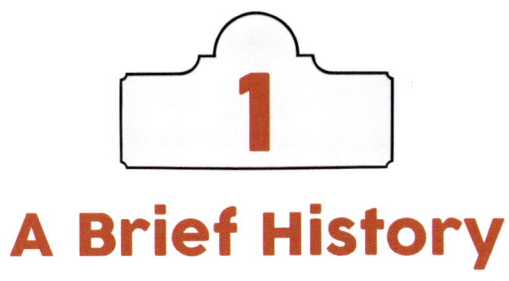

A Brief History

150 million years ago, before humans evolved, dinosaurs and other reptiles trudged around large freshwater lakes which would have covered much of modern-day East Sussex. We know that rhinoceros and elephants grazed in what is now Eastbourne as the bones of these creatures have been discovered in South Street and near Grove Road.

The tidal effects of various ice ages meant that southern England was often covered with a thick layer of inhospitable ice but, as it rescinded, animals and, about 200,000 years ago, humans settled. The earliest human activity in Eastbourne dates from this Palaeolithic (old-stone) Age. This is evidenced by many flint implements found nearby. These early settlers would have shared their life with rhinoceros and elephants and remains of these creatures have been found in South Street and near Grove Road.

As the weather again became colder our early occupants and the wildlife would have retreated back onto what is now mainland Europe; however the last ice age was about 12,000 years ago and didn't quite reach Eastbourne. Man was here to stay.

Over thousands of years flint tools slowly became more refined. Settlements became larger and more permanent. Hunting and fishing could be hit and miss so a more reliable source of food became prevalent – farming. Early farmers started to clear woodlands and also domesticated animals such as cattle. Agriculture led to more sophisticated methods of cooking and earthenware pottery was made.

It is in the Neolithic period of about 6,000 years ago when local groups protected themselves by building embankments around their settlements – known as causewayed enclosures. There were several in the area including Belle Tout, Willingdon and Seaford. Artifacts found in the Eastbourne area include 'Peterborough-ware' pottery and a handaxe made in North Wales (Graig Lwyd, near Colwyn Bay), which show that there was considerable movement and trading between Eastbourne and the whole country.

The knowledge of using and making metal for tools arrived from mainland Europe about 4,000 years ago when the Bronze Age began. In 1995 a significant settlement from this period was discovered at the newly created Shinewater Neighbourhood Park. Excavations revealed wooden platforms and trackways

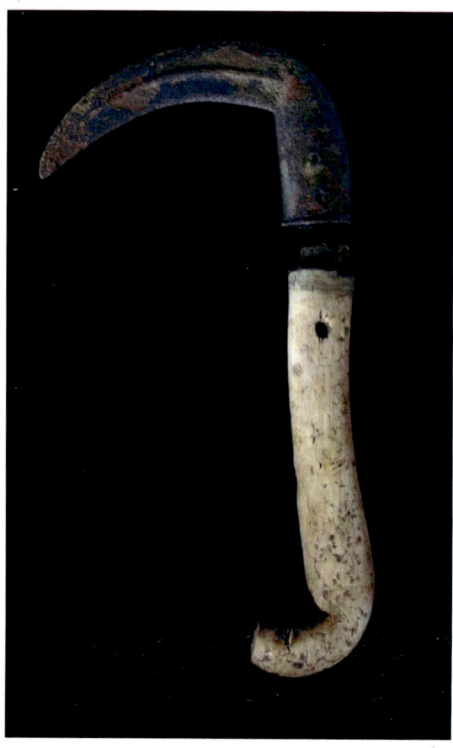

The sickle found at Shinewater.
(Heritage Eastbourne)

held up by vertical posts. The village would have stood above brackish waters, so fresh water would have had to have been brought in. Raised clay hearths and a sickle (with wooden handle intact) were found and as some pottery was dated to over 2,000 years ago it is likely that this settlement was considerable in size and duration.

There would have been other settlements around. Iron Age pottery from 2,000 years ago was once found in Green Street and, as some of it was disfigured and discarded during firing, it was clearly made here.

About 2,500 years ago tribes from northern Gaul (France) started to arrive in the east of England. These 'Belgae' settlers gradually moved south and occupied our coast. They were well-organised and were led by kings. They used money and their coins have been found locally. The tribe that occupied the Eastbourne area were known as the 'Regni'.

The Regni had close links with the Roman Empire and when the Romans invaded in AD 43 there would have been little local resistance; indeed the invading army may have been welcomed. A new local king was installed called Tiberius Cladius Cogidubnus. He probably resided at the huge and beautifully decorated villa at Fishbourne near Chichester. His local representatives had villas across the area and one of these was at Eastbourne. The Eastbourne villa was in the area of the pier and the Burlington Hotel and included a substantial bath and decorated pavements.

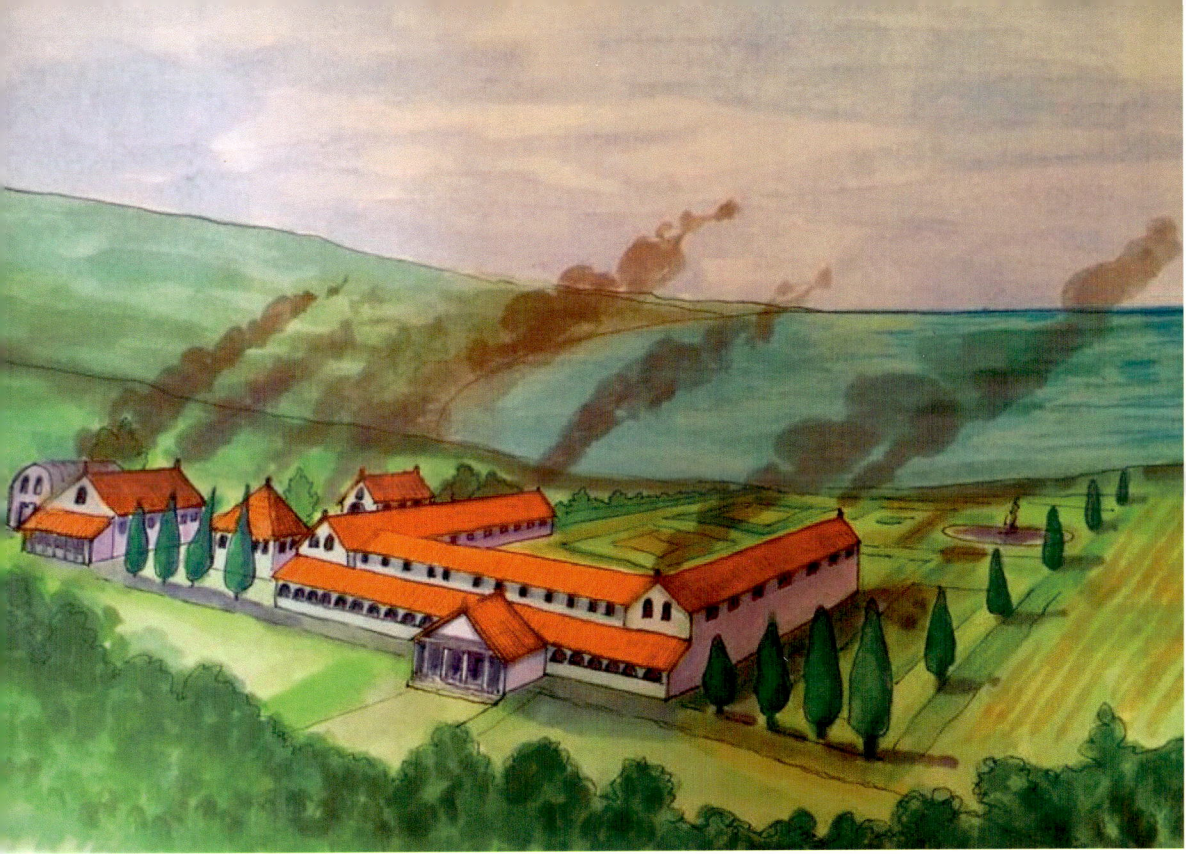

Eastbourne Roman Villa. (Helen Greaves-Warren)

One of Eastbourne's Roman residents was a twenty-four-year-old woman about 5 feet tall. She was buried on the Downs above Eastbourne and anthropologists believe she was born in the south-eastern area of the Mediterranean, maybe north Africa. The DNA used to identify her was extracted from one of her teeth and this is celebrated by the tooth-shaped beach hut erected on the seafront. The Roman occupation bought new technology and farming methods and probably considerable wealth to the area. There was a Roman village at Arlington (now lost under the reservoir) whose occupants would have ploughed the surrounding countryside and would have travelled to Eastbourne and other settlements by newly laid roads.

As the Roman Empire started to crumble, the Saxons from northern Germany began to attack our coast and the Romans built a series of forts for protection. One of these at Anderida became Pevensey Castle and Roman tiles are still evident at the base of its stocky walls.

By the year 500 the Saxons had invaded the whole area, which became the Kingdom of the Sudsexe (South Saxons and now Sussex).

In Eastbourne, the Saxons occupied the ridge of what is now Willingdon Road and burials from the time have been found there. Excavations evidenced another import into the country in the form of Christianity. St Wilfrid had arrived in Sussex in the year 670 and he surely visited the area, although may not have

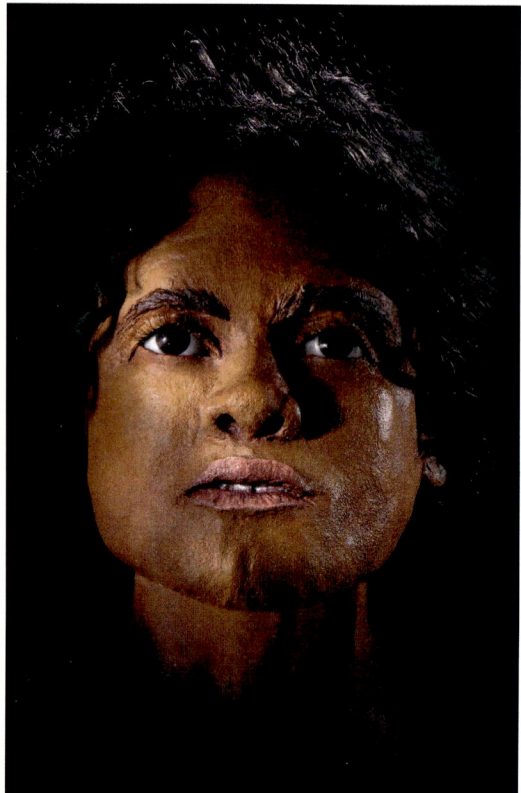 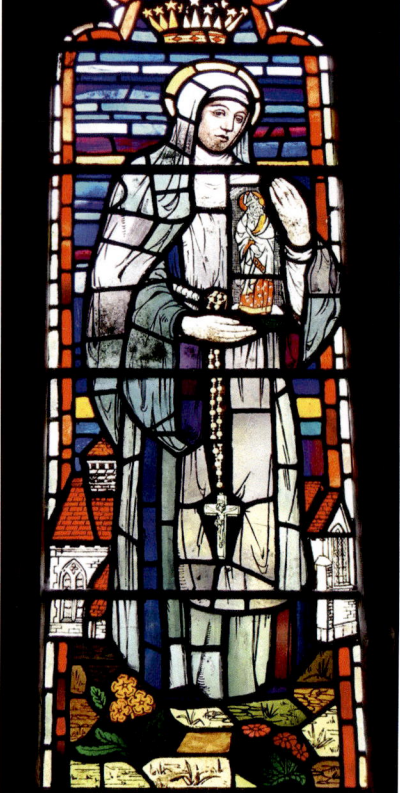

Above left: Eastbourne's Roman resident. (Heritage Eastbourne)

Above right: St Lewinna shown here in a stained-glass window at Brede church.

been too welcome. Five years later a young girl at nearby Seaford was killed for her Christian beliefs and is now our local saint, St Lewinna. There was an early wooden church (dedicated to St Michael) at Eastbourne but no evidence now remains.

The Saxons increased in numbers and many of our local villages bear names of Saxon origin including those that contain 'ing', 'ham', 'hurst', 'ton' and 'wick'. It was about this time that Eastbourne got its name 'Bourne' from the stream, which rose from a series of freshwater wells in what is now known as Motcombe. The Saxons had an early form of local government which assembled at a meeting place or moot. It is probable that the field (or croft) where this happened is now in the area called Moatcroft Road. Leading men started to claim land and used people to farm it. They became 'Lords of the Manor'.

Around the year 900 there were a number of Viking raids on the south coast but they did not settle here and the next invasion was not until 28 September 1066. Local librarian and Eastbourne historian Alfred Ensor wrote in 1976, 'One can imagine the anxiety with which the sharper-eyed Saxons on high-points of

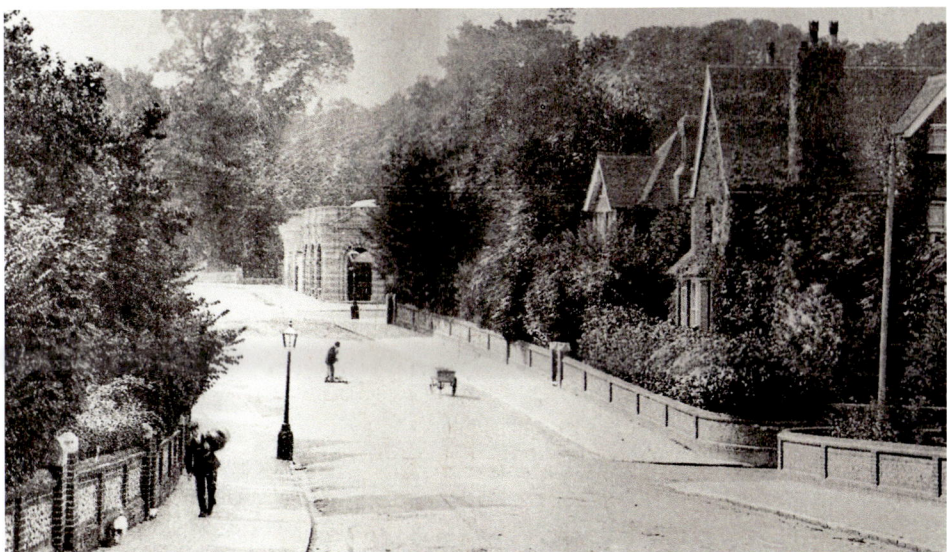

Moatcroft Road.

the Downs watched the invaders and the relief they that they must have felt when it became apparent that the army was turning eastwards towards Hastings and not westwards towards Eastbourne. The news of the battle and the defeat of the Saxon Army must have left them puzzled and apprehensive.'

William the Conqueror safeguarded his invasion beachhead by giving the nearby land to his brother Robert, Count of Mortain, and to protect it he enlarged the old Roman port and fort at Pevensey. The conqueror's census, the Domesday Book of 1086, shows that Eastbourne was a substantial village of about 300 to 400 people which, before the Norman invasion, was owned by King Edward the Confessor. There was a watermill, saltpans and probably a tide mill. There may have been a small harbour close to what is now the Wish Tower. Of course the largest building to be constructed in Eastbourne by the Normans was its church but more about that in Chapter 3.

The countryside around the church was surrounded by large fields which in Sussex were called 'laines'. These were owned by the lord of the manor and were split into long allotment-like strips which were rented out to villagers. Each man was given several strips to farm, often in different areas so everyone had a share of good and bad land. Although the rent for the strips was relatively low, the men had to work a certain amount of days on the lands owned by the local lord. Tenants would also have to serve the lord in other ways including protecting him and his land, sometimes militarily. Some tenants at Eastbourne had to take their turn working at Pevensey Castle.

After the Norman invasion, the old Saxon manors were handed over to the Count of Mortain, who gave them to his friends. These landlords were usually absent but were happy to profit from rents and agricultural yields. This feudal

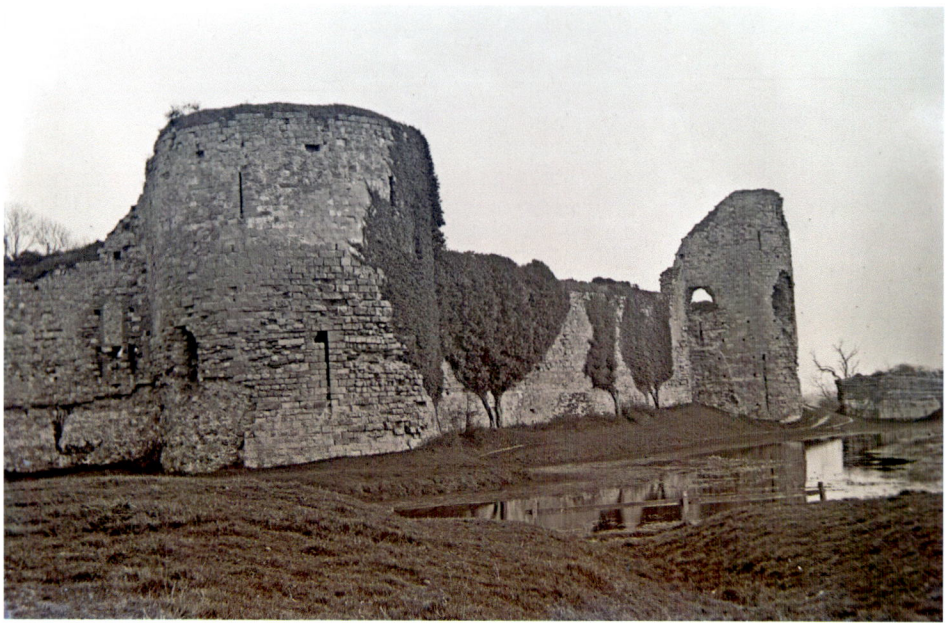

system was the norm in Eastbourne for many years, with bailiffs collecting rents and fining the tenants where necessary.

Things changed with the Black Death of the fourteenth century. About one-third of the population of Eastbourne died and there was no longer a sufficient workforce to grow and harvest crops. When there is a shortage of manpower, salaries rise to the annoyance of employers – the landowners. The government's lawyers tried to introduce wage controls, which was the background of the Peasants Revolt of 1450 led by Sussex-born Jack Cade.

Shakespeare wrote about the rebellion in his play *Henry VI Part II*. One of the rebels is called Dick, who urges Jack Cade to 'Kill all the lawyers'. Dick has been identified as Richard Burton, one of three men from Eastbourne known to have participated in the uprising. Burton was eventually pardoned by Henry VI and returned home.

In 1555 the manor of Eastbourne was sold by another absentee landlord, Henry Manvers, 2nd Earl of Rutland. To make the sale profitable, the manor of Eastbourne was split into three parts. John Burton (a descendent of the rebellious Dick) bought Meads and much of what is now the town centre. He lived in Bourne Place. John Selwyn took the north of the town and the family initially lived at Motcombe Farm but went on to occupy Ratton Manor. Thomas Gildredge bought the eastern area of the town, which included Upperton. His family settled in the fifteenth-century Eastbourne Manor House, which can still be seen in the Goffs.

Over subsequent generations the owners of these three new manors went on to be influential in the development of Eastbourne.

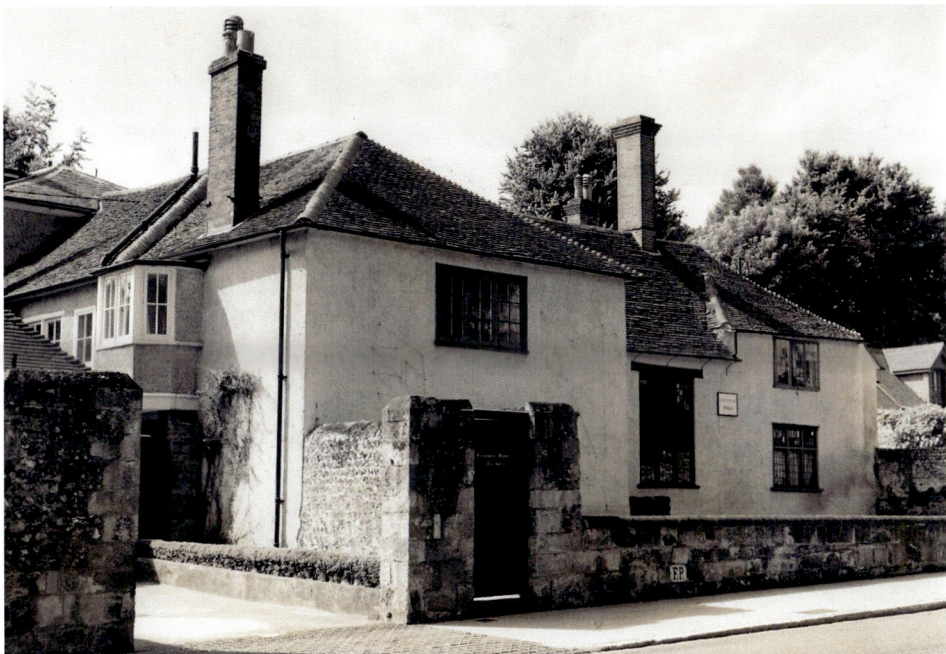

The Manor House in the Goffs.

In 1723 the Burton family sold up to the Honourable Spencer Compton and Bourne Place became Compton Place. Lady Betty Compton married George Cavendish, 1st Earl of Burlington, in 1782. He was the son of the 4th Duke of Devonshire and the Eastbourne estates soon passed to the Dukes of Devonshire. They still own Compton Place and much of Eastbourne and in the late nineteenth century their money transformed the town from a fishing village into a seaside resort.

Over time the Gildredge estates were bequeathed to the Gilbert family, who are still based nearby at East Dean.

Now that is an awful lot of history, but these families are still celebrated in Eastbourne with streets, hotels and even pubs named after them. The families are also remembered in Eastbourne's coat of arms, which were granted to Eastbourne by the Royal College of Arms on 11 January 1928. However, it is clear that the crest and motto were used unofficially before this time.

Officially the coat of arms are: 'Argent on a fesse double cottised Gules a Rose Or between two stag's heads caboshed in the field'. This basically means red stripes on a silver background with two stag's heads either side of a gold rose. The crest is a green seahorse raising his right foot (a bit odd considering that seahorses don't have feet!). The stag's heads are from the Cavendish coat of arms and the rose appears on the Gilbert coat of arms.

The Eastbourne motto 'MELIORA SEQUIMUR' roughly translates as 'We strive for higher things', although it has also been translated as 'Let us look for something better' (which, to be honest, is not a good motto for a holiday resort).

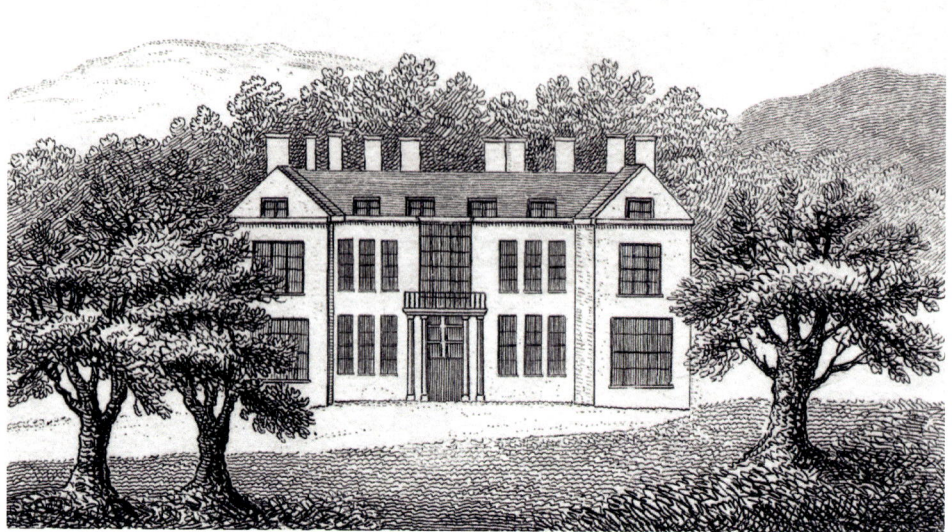

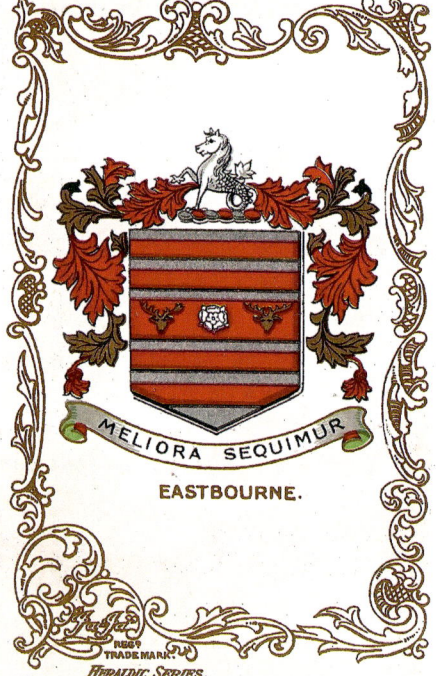

Above: Compton Place.

Left: Eastbourne's coat of arms.

Interestingly a report appeared in the *Dundee Evening Telegraph* of January 1948 saying that the Eastbourne coat of arms was bogus and that the people of Eastbourne should be embarrassed. In the following edition a letter from Eastbourne's Director of Publicity put them right.

Talking about publicity, what do people say about Eastbourne?

Eastbourne Reviewed

'This little bathing-place is thronged with families of the first distinction. The theatre is well attended and a ball at the Lamb Inn recently boasted an overflow of fashionable company. The parade is delightfully situated close to the sea and the bands of the Surrey and Shropshire regiments, which are based here, play every evening.'

The Globe, 1809

'Eastbourne consists of four detached parts, two of which, Seahouses and Meades are near the sea. The others are South Bourne and East Bourne which is about a mile and a half from the sea. In late years it has become a fashionable bathing place.'

Beauties of England and Wales, 1813

'Eastbourne is the dullest of watering places.'

Charles Lamb, *Poor Relations*, 1823

'The delightfully retired village of Eastbourne continues to hold a pre-eminent rank in the catalogue of highly favoured watering places and it is certainly not surprising that Eastbourne should be selected as a chosen retirement during the summer from the noisy and bustling scenes of the gay and swarming metropolis. The salubrity of the air, the extraordinary purity and excellence of the water are in themselves sufficient points of attraction, and, when combined with the beautiful rides and walks with which Eastbourne abound, we do not hesitate to pronounce that it soars above its rivals.'

Sussex Advertiser, 1824

'In 1821 the population of Eastbourne numbered only 2,607 inhabitants but now it probably has nearly 10,000. The causes of this rapid increase are; the known

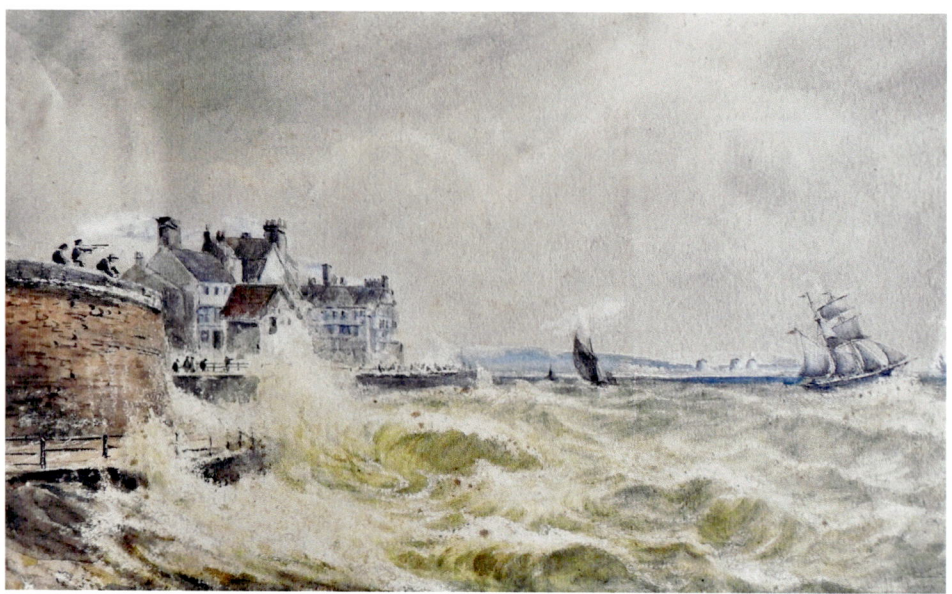

salubrity of the place, its picturesque scenery both landward and seaward, and thirdly railway accommodation which brings it within two hours of London. Thus, what was a century ago little more than a rude fishing village, is now a very fashionable and important watering-place.'

Mark Antony Lower,
The History of Sussex, 1870

'Thirty years ago the flanks of the Downs and the broad plain between them and the sea, close under the shadow of Beachy Head, the land was dotted with cottages grouped into three villages. A new town of stately character has sprung up called EASTBOURNE. Here, there are a succession of good houses with parades and terraces among the finest in Europe.'

George Moseley, *Eastbourne as a Residence for Invalids and Winter Resort*, 1882

'Eastbourne is the most select of Sussex watering places. Hastings is 'of the people' Brighton is continental but Eastbourne is select. Lawn Tennis and golf are its staple products and it is an admirable town for horsemanship.'

Frederick Griggs,
Highways and Byways of Sussex, 1904

'One of the cleanest, best laid-out and most charming of the big seaside resorts in the country.'

S. P. B. Mais, 1929

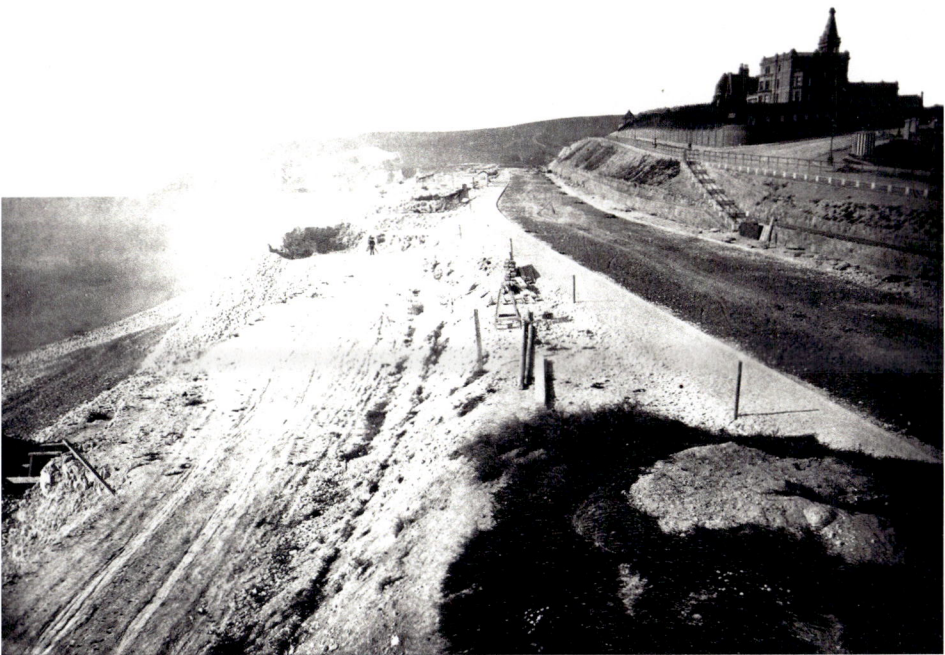

The Parades being laid out.

'Eastbourne has the finest approach in England if we come to it from the Downs; it has the finest seaside front, unique for its natural splendour and blaze of summer glory. It has tree lined avenues and spacious streets and there is no seaside place in England better laid out than this beautiful town'.

Arthur Mee, *Sussex*, 1937

'Eastbourne is famed for its schools and excellent sporting facilities. It is a young town which a hundred years ago boasted only a few houses on what is now Marine Parade. Since then it has grown to become the third largest town in Sussex thanks largely to the good taste of the former Dukes of Devonshire upon whose land much of Eastbourne is built. It is an extremely well laid out town and its Corporation are keenly appreciative of the beauty of the South Downs to its west and are zealous to safeguard it.'

Norman Wymer, *Companion to Sussex*, 1950

'Eastbourne and excitement are foreign to each other.'

Spike Milligan, *Adolf Hitler: My Part in his Downfall*, 1971

But that is all in the past – what of the town now?

'Today it retains its genteel feel, with neatly manicured gardens, an annual ATP tennis tournament and a pretty pier. But a fresh energy is bubbling up too, as the next generation of thirty-somethings make a move here. Independent coffee shops and cafés are springing up and there's a collaborative mindset among the arts crowd as Eastbourne slowly begins to evolve once more.'

Emma Love, *Conde Nast Traveller*, 2021

'Eastbourne doesn't deserve the 'Gods Waiting Room' rap; as more families are lured to life by the seaside, the average age in the town is 45. Since 1992 yachties have been drawn to the town with the opening of the Sovereign Harbour, northern Europe's largest marina complex. On a fine day you could be in the South of France. In 2009 the Towner Art Gallery relocated to a striking new building, the largest purpose built gallery in the south-east. It has received accolades and prizes for its bold architecture and in 2020 was the Art Fund's Museum of the Year.'

Jeannine Williamson, *The Independent*, 2021

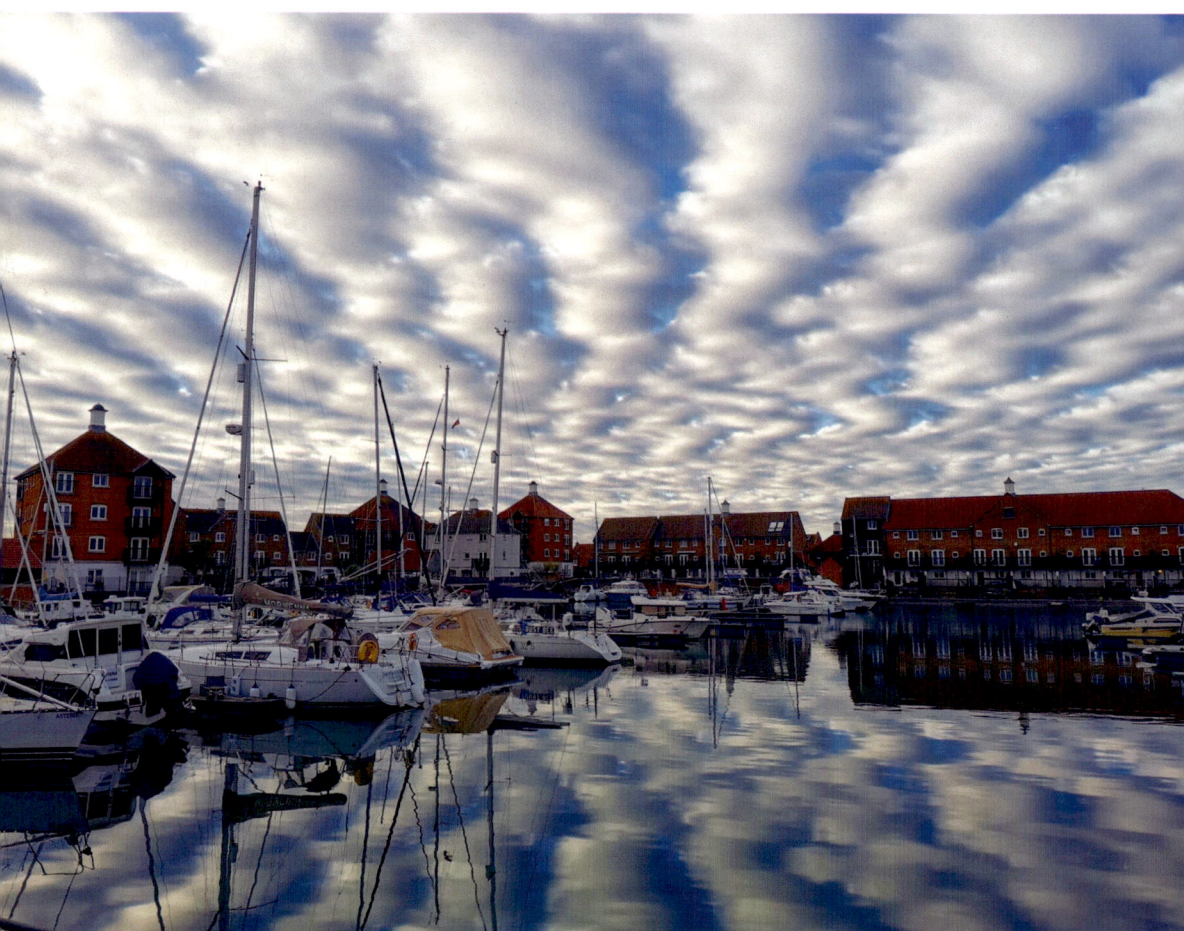

Sovereign Harbour.

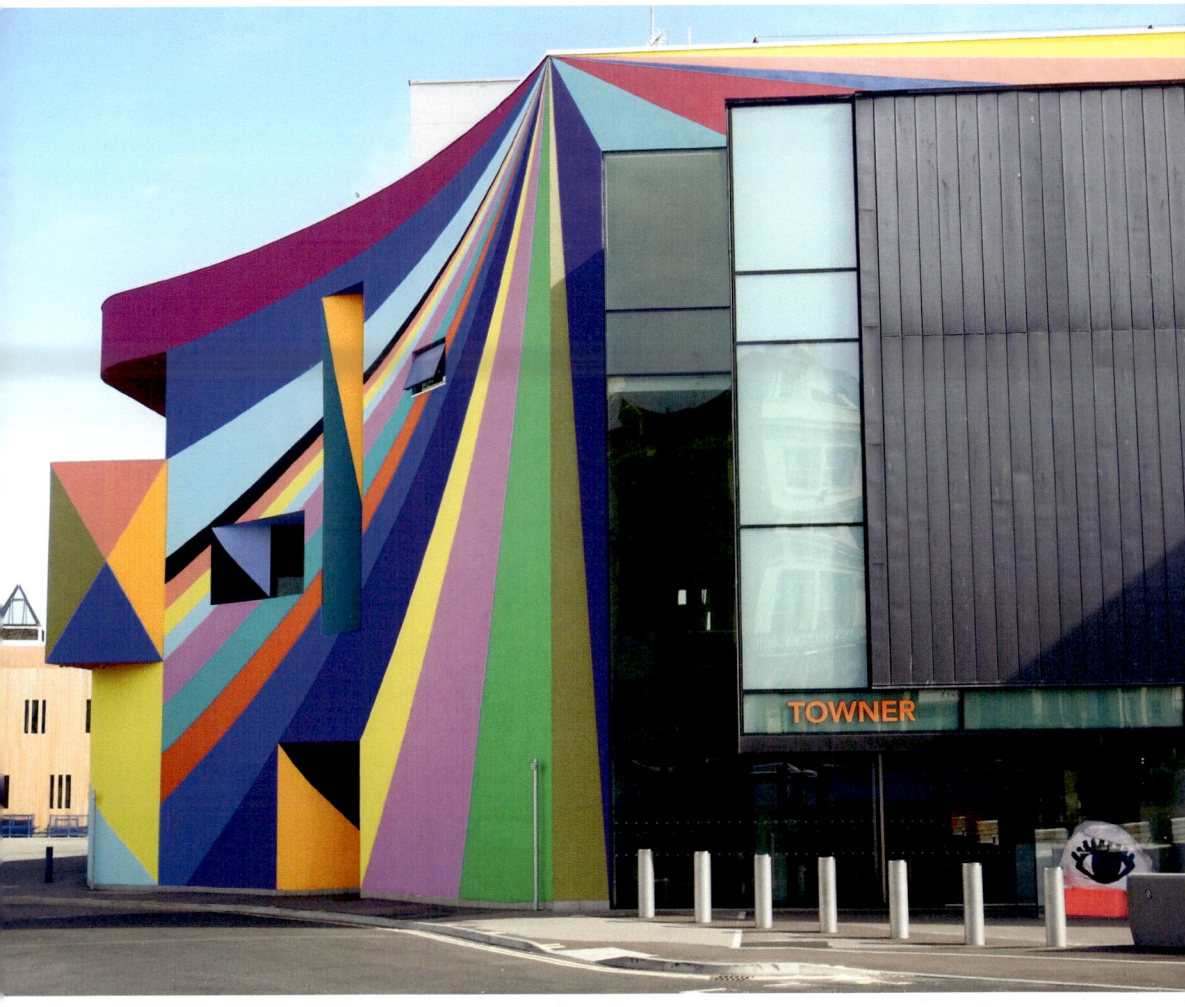

The Towner Art Gallery.

Before we consider modern Eastbourne, let's look at its past.

The Church

'St Mary's is an ancient building consisting of a lofty nave with two spacious aisles, a large chancel and an antique tower with a peal of eight bells. The style of the church is chiefly early gothic although some windows are decidedly Norman. The old unsightly pews have given place to modern ones and the once cold building is made comfortable by hot air and in place of gloomy candles, gas now gives a cheerful light.'

Herbert's Guide to Eastbourne, 1871

St Mary's Church.

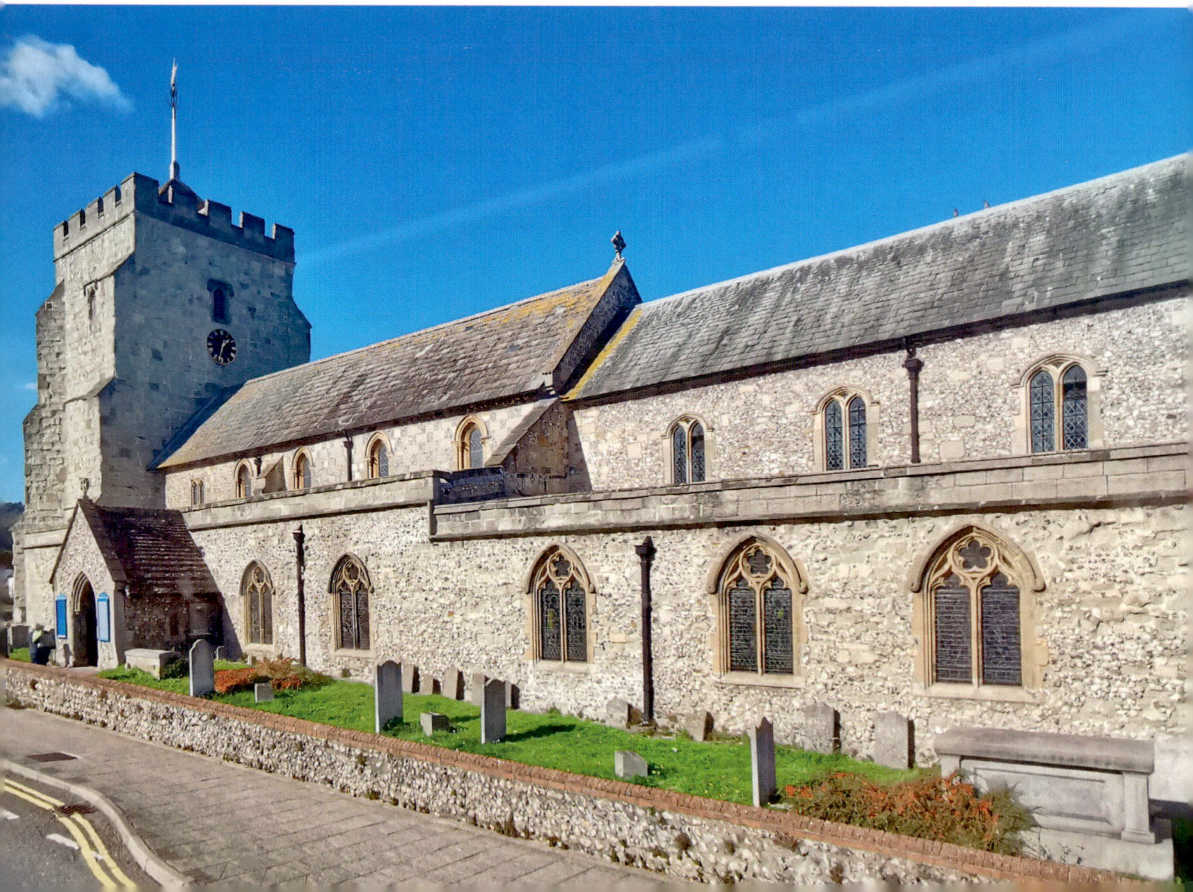

The heart of most communities is its church and the parish church of St Mary the Virgin in Old Town is no exception. There has been a church here since the eleventh century. There may well have been an earlier wooden Saxon church, possibly dedicated to St Michael, on the ridge of Ocklynge Hill close to the present-day St Michael and All Angels Church but no trace of this Saxon building has been discovered.

St Mary's Church bells were first installed in 1651 and have proudly and loudly rung out across the centuries to draw its congregation to worship and to celebrate local weddings and national events.

The church is open every day and welcomes visitors. It is well worth a visit to a church which has much to see – from ancient 'guild' chapels to graffiti.

When you first enter the church you are immediately struck by how massive it is, which is surprising when you consider that, when it was first built, the village of 'Bourne' would have not been much bigger than most other villages under the Sussex Downs. It was built under the guidance of William Neville, the treasurer of Chichester Cathedral around 1160. The cathedral clearly wanted to benefit from church revenues, not only the tithes from the surrounding farmland, but also those collected from the local fishermen. A tithe was a statutory 10 per cent tax paid to support the church. In rural areas it could also be paid in goods. In 1341 Eastbourne church received tithes which included hay, rushes, calves and milk, but it would also include a portion of a fisherman's catch. The tithe paid by local fishermen was called a 'Christ-share'. There were barns to the north of the church,

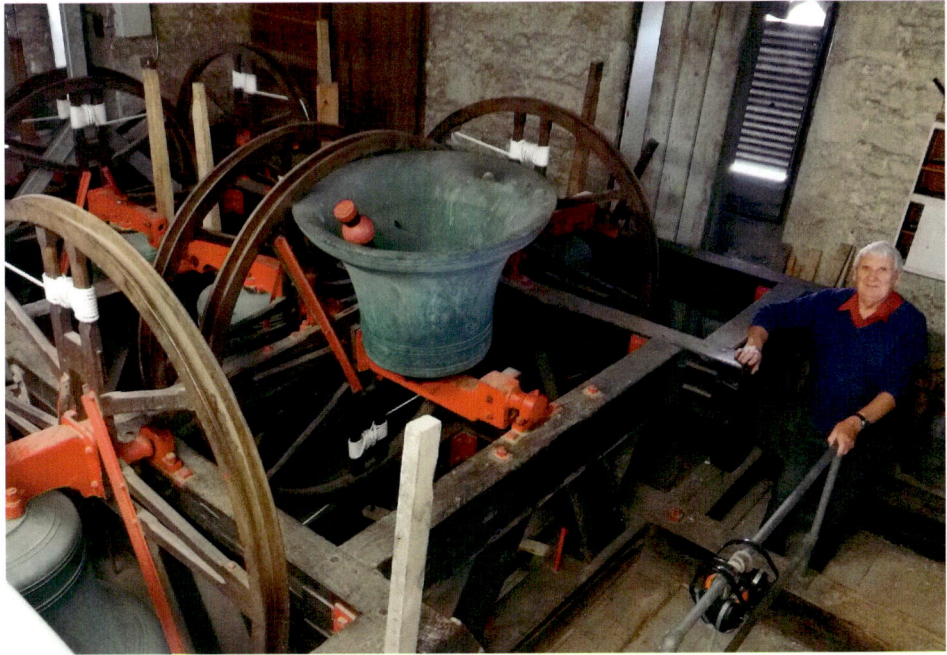

St Mary's Church bells.

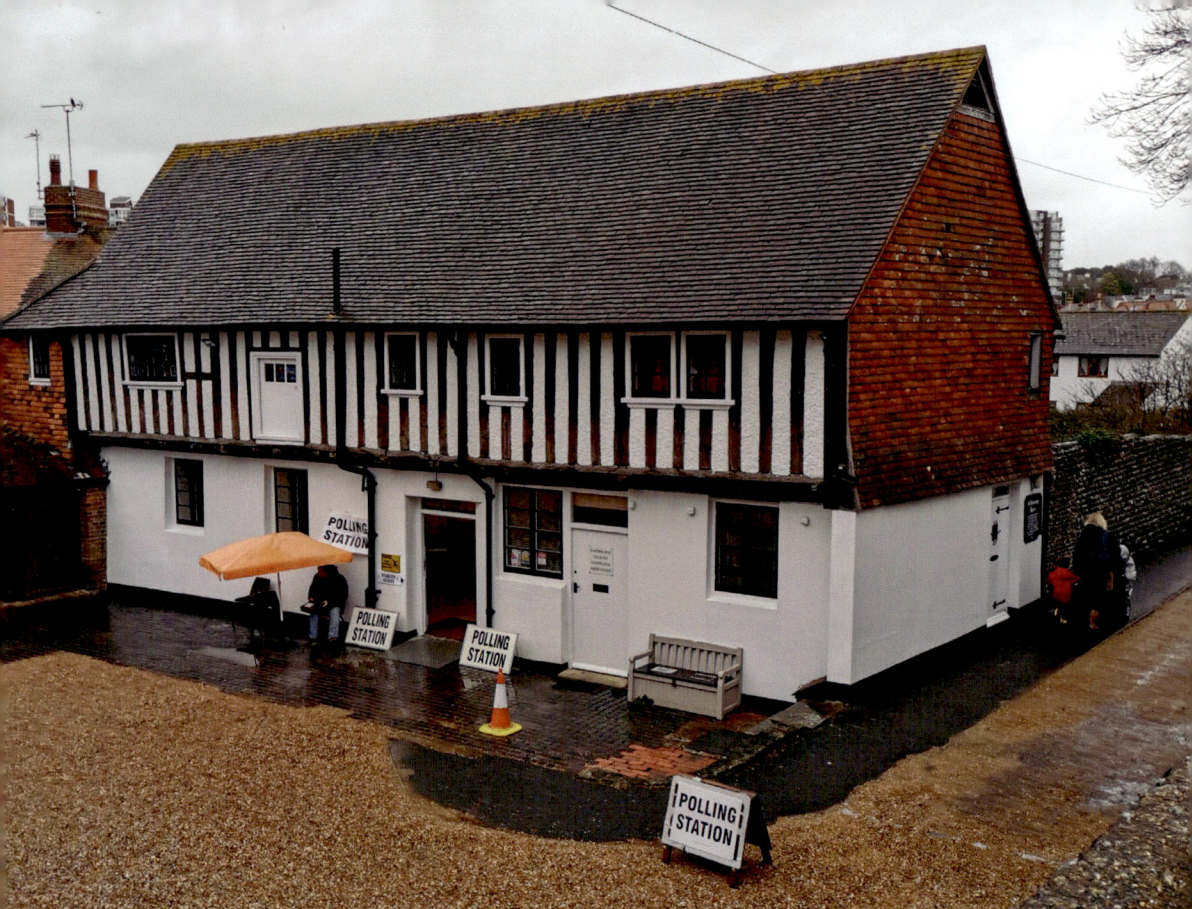

Parsonage barn.

one of which, 'Parsonage Barn', is still in-situ and these would have been used to store the tithes. Chichester cathedral must have benefitted well from tithes, the tithe barn at nearby Alciston is one of the largest in England.

As you stand in the nave of the church looking east towards the altar you will notice that the north and south aisles are separated by massive green-sandstone columns alternately round and octagonal. Now walk down the right-hand (south) aisle. A door on the left, watched over by a friendly face with a bulbous nose, once led to a long-lost tower. A number of side chapels were once located in this aisle. They were dedicated to St Richard of Chichester, St Michael, St Mary and St Seithe (an Italian saint also known as St Zita invoked for people who lost their keys). These were Guild Chapels and the largest was probably for the Guild or Brotherhood of Jesus as they also owned a large building on the other side of Church Street. These guilds were similar to later 'friendly societies' and would have supported their members, and the church, in times of difficulty.

Evidence of these ancient chapels can be seen in the eight wooden screens in the south aisle, which have been dated from 1315 to 1350. One of them has some scratched graffiti in the form of a ship in full sail. Was this done by a sailor, happy to have survived a treacherous journey, or by a cheeky bored choirboy?

As you pass along towards the altar have a close look at the octagonal column on your right. Scratched into the ancient stone are three fish drawn vertically. They are not too clear but using the light from your mobile phone may help to see them.

It has always been known that there was medieval graffiti at St Mary's Church but it was not until a full survey led by local archaeologist Jo Seaman that the full extent of the graffiti was discovered. There are nearly 300 examples in the church but what were once considered 'masons marks' probably have a deeper meaning. A closer look shows that many of the 'fish' seem to have 'beaks' and look more like dolphins. Dolphins were a good omen for fishermen and were believed to help lost sailors find the shore. The dolphin could be a representation of Christian salvation – the maritime version of the holy lamb in Christian art.

To the right of the altar are the sedilia. This tall, Gothic arched feature, installed in the mid-fourteenth century to provide seats for the clergy, cuts through one of the scratched fish, which gives us a clue as to how long ago it was drawn. On the other side to the left of the altar is an Easter Sepulchre. This represents the tomb where Jesus was laid after his crucifixion and they are only found in England and Wales. As it was only used for three days a year, an Easter Sepulchre was often made of wood and few survive but in some churches such as nearby Alfriston it was made of stone and built into the chancel to the north of the altar. At Easter the consecrated host (representing the body of Jesus) would be placed in the Sepulchre on Maundy Thursday and guarded by a succession of parishioners until Easter Sunday when it would be taken out and placed back on the altar. This represented Christ having arisen from the tomb.

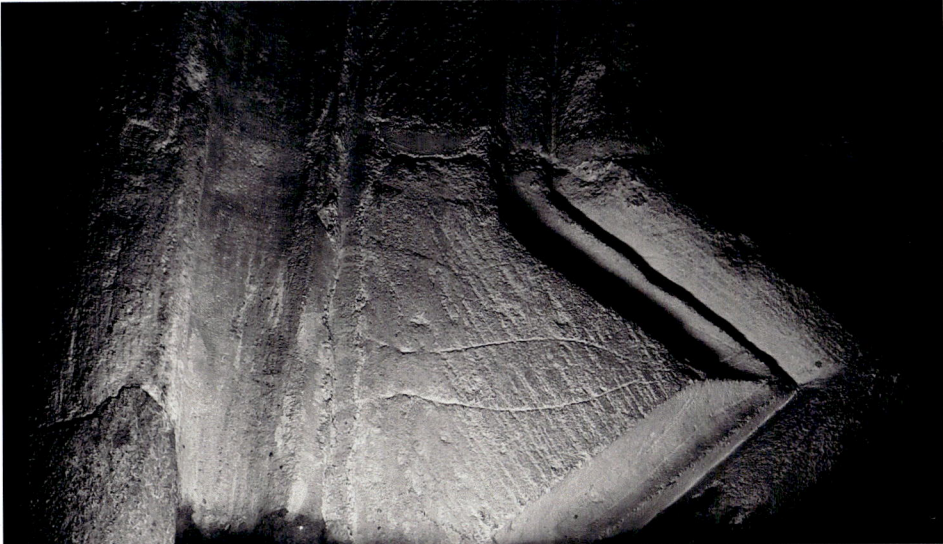

Church graffiti.

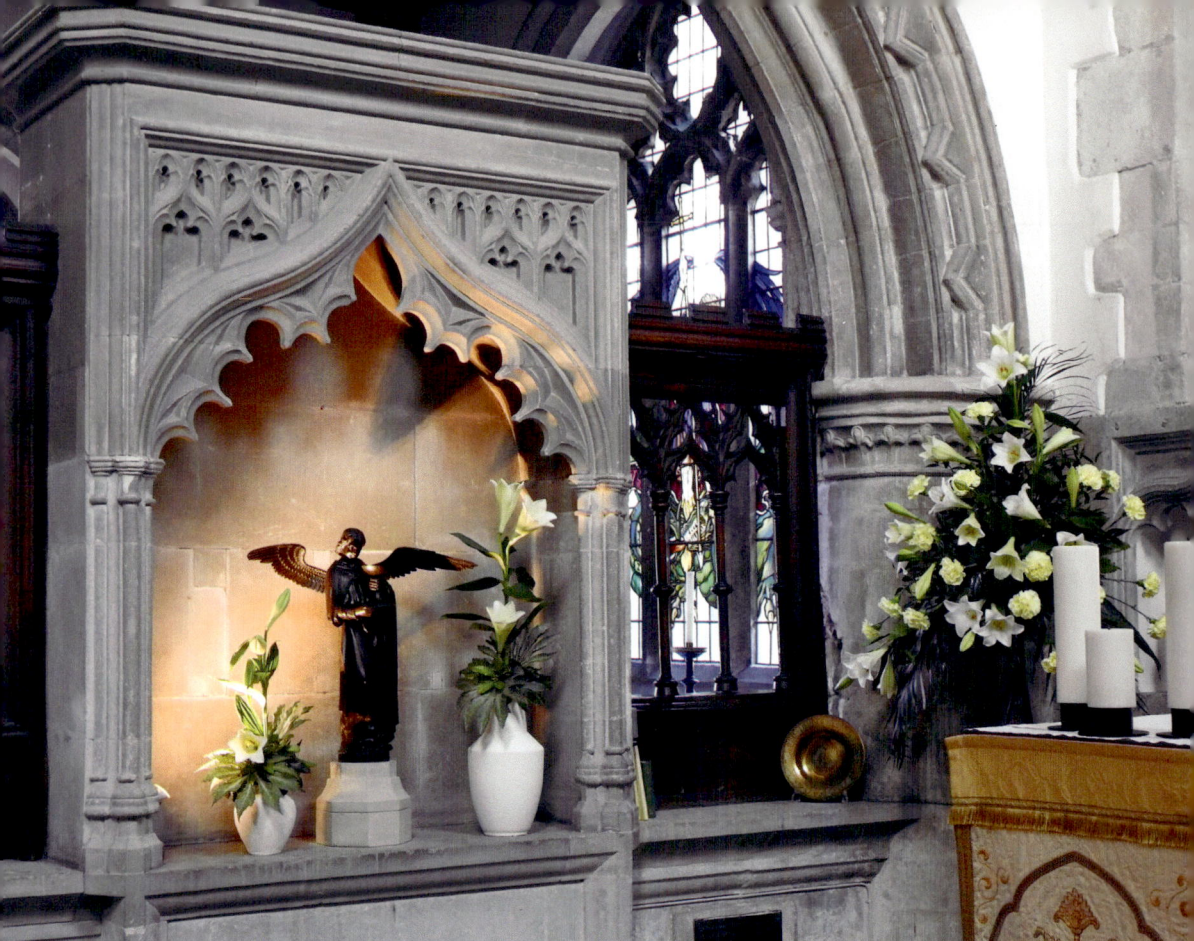

Easter Sepulchre.

Turn and look back up the church. On either side ahead of you are the choir stalls. High on the left-hand (south) wall are three large diamond-shaped funeral hatchments. Funeral hatchments would depict a family coat of arms so would only be used by the gentry. After a funeral or memorial service they were nailed above the front door of the family home to show that the house was in mourning. After a period of mourning, which could be up to six months, they were sometimes displayed in the parish church.

Take a look at the closest one with the motto 'Cavendo Tutus' or 'Be safe' – a nice play on words with the surname Cavendish. It is for George Cavendish, 1st Earl of Burlington. He lived in Burlington House in Piccadilly and was the chap who built Burlington Arcade. Now with a funeral hatchment, the left-hand side is for the husband and the right-hand side is for the wife. Note how George's side is black whereas his wife (Elizabeth's) side is white. This means that he died before her.

Take a look at the centre hatchment. Can you see that the right-hand side has a white background but the 'wife's side' has a black background? This means that she died before him. This is the hatchment for Blanche, the wife of the 7th Duke of

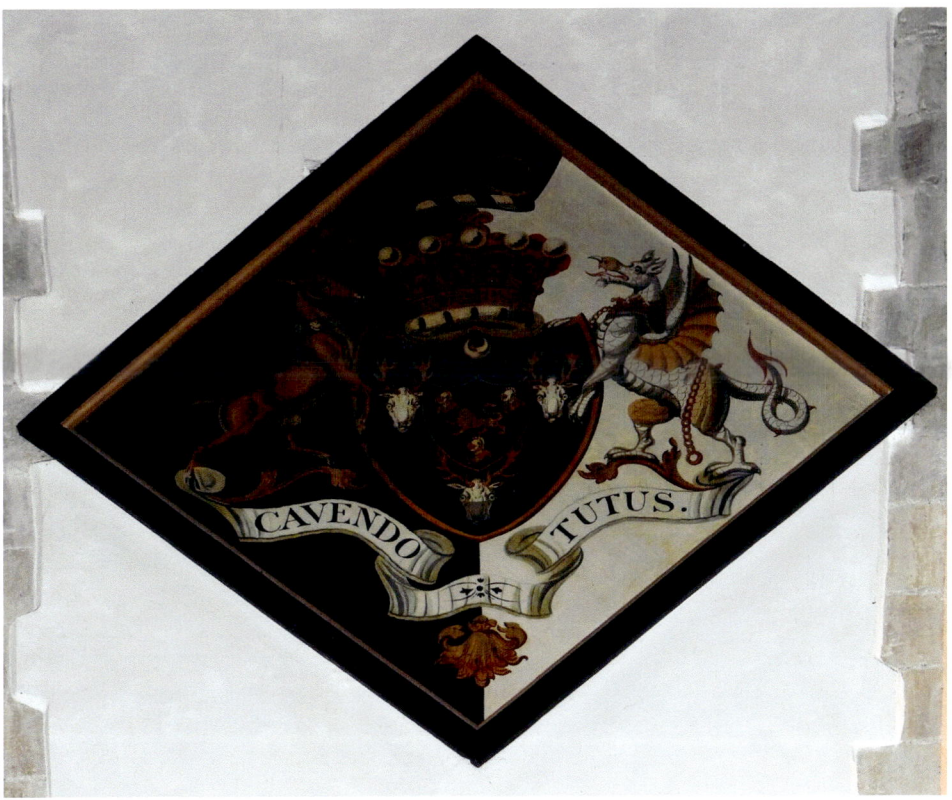

Cavendish funeral hatchment.

Devonshire, the man who put much of his family money into the development of Victorian Eastbourne. Blanche was just seventeen when she met William and they married soon afterwards. She was a 'Lady of the Bedchamber' for Queen Victoria. The marriage to William was to be short lived as she died in her late twenties, just ten years later.

The third hatchment is for Elizabeth Cavendish, the wife of George, 1st Earl of Burlington. All three would have at one time been displayed above the porch at Compton Place.

On the opposite (north) wall are two square royal coats of arms. The closer one is for Queen Elizabeth II, who worshipped here on a number of occasions as a child whilst staying at Compton Place. The further one is for George III and originally faced the congregation over the chancel arch as a reminder that the king was the head of the Church of England. The arms were donated to the church by the Gilbert family and you can just see their coat of arms at the base – a red chevron surmounted a nut-eating squirrel.

Walk ahead into the north aisle. The chapel to the right has many memorials for the Gilbert and Gildredge families. As you walk up the north aisle you will see on your right a monument with an anchor. This is the memorial for Lieutenant

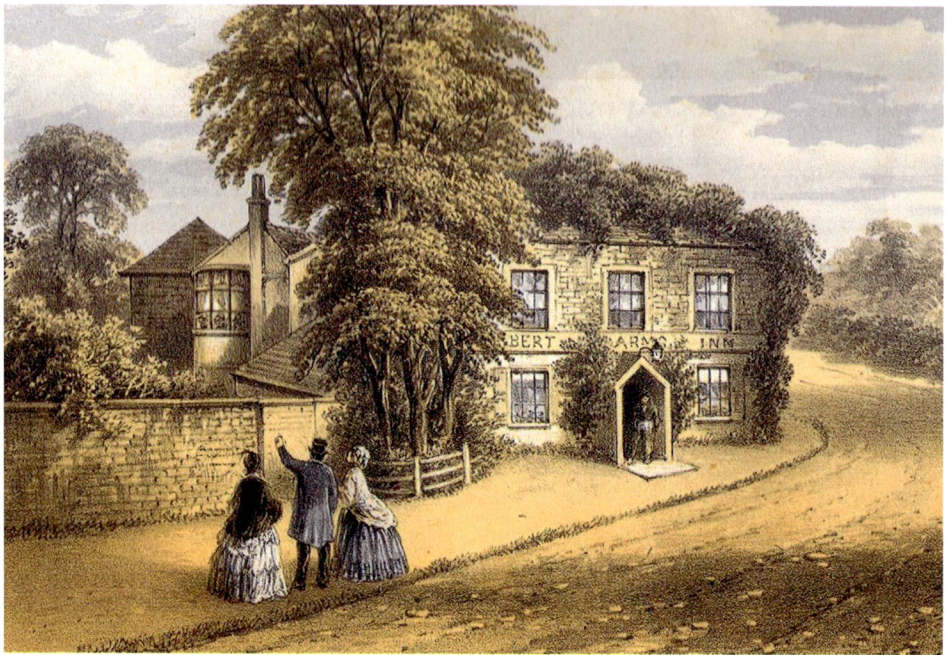

The Squirrel Inn.

There was once a prominent pub near the railway station called the Gilbert Arms but, because it displayed the Gilbert coat-of arms, it was known by the locals as 'The Squirrel'. The inn had rooms and was regularly used by Sir William Sterndale Bennett (1816–1875) the composer famous for his '*May Queen*'. He was a favourite of Queen Victoria and was once described by the New York Times as '*probably the greatest composer produced by England*'. The Eastbourne Choral Society was established in 1877 and they practised in the Pavilion at Devonshire Park with one of its first concerts being '*The May Queen*'.

William Rason, who was killed during a skirmish in the Chinese Opium Wars. He was the captain of HMS *Plover*, and he lost his head (literally) in 1859 during an action which was noted as the first occasion that the British fought alongside American forces. The anchor on the memorial is actually made from metal from HMS *Plover*.

Continue walking up the north aisle and stop by the round column close to the north door. Again you need to use your mobile-phone torch and rake it across the surface. You will see two examples of 'daisy-wheel' graffiti. The scratch marks of concentric circles are again of unknown origin. On a secular building they can be interpreted as 'witches marks' used as ritual

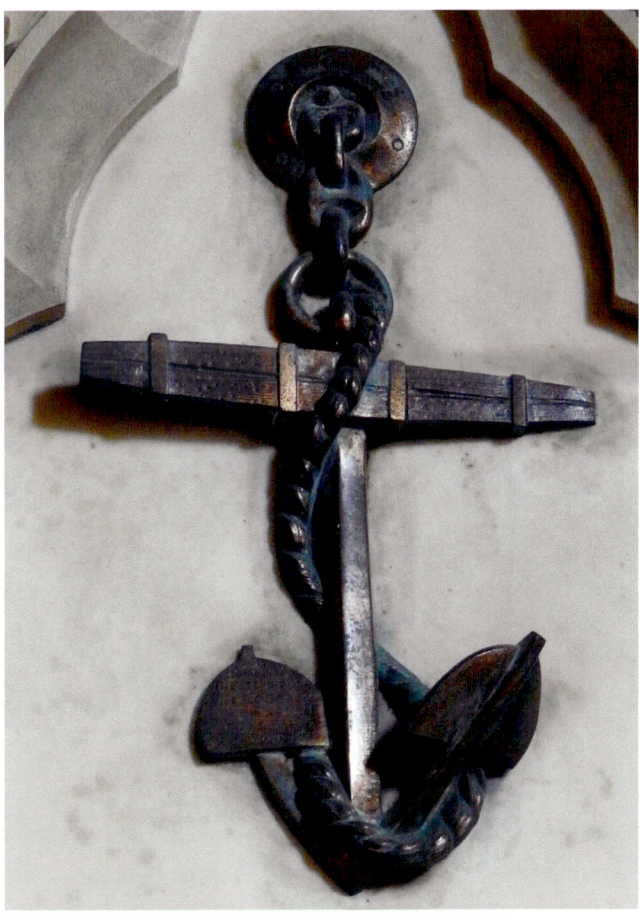

The Rason Anchor.

protection against evil but surely a church does not need these? They were first recorded in 1912 but have recently been carefully photographed as part of the church graffiti project.

On the south nave wall near the tower you will see a memorial on the left to Alexander Brodie and his wife Anna. History books praise Alexander for his short tenure as vicar of the church between 1809 and 1828 but little is written about his wife Anna, who even gets short shrift on this memorial. The truth is she was a far more interesting character than her husband.

Until 1817 Alexander Brodie held land and owned slaves on a sugar plantation in Antigua. This would have given him a good income but his wife received far more money as she had shares in *The Times* newspaper, which had been established as *The Daily Universal Register* by her father, John Walter. Not only did Anna have shares but she was virtually running the paper in the 1820s when it was estimated that she (and another partner) were making up to £30,000 a year from sales. Today that that would be an annual income of some £6 million!

The Brodie family lived at the Gore in Upperton.

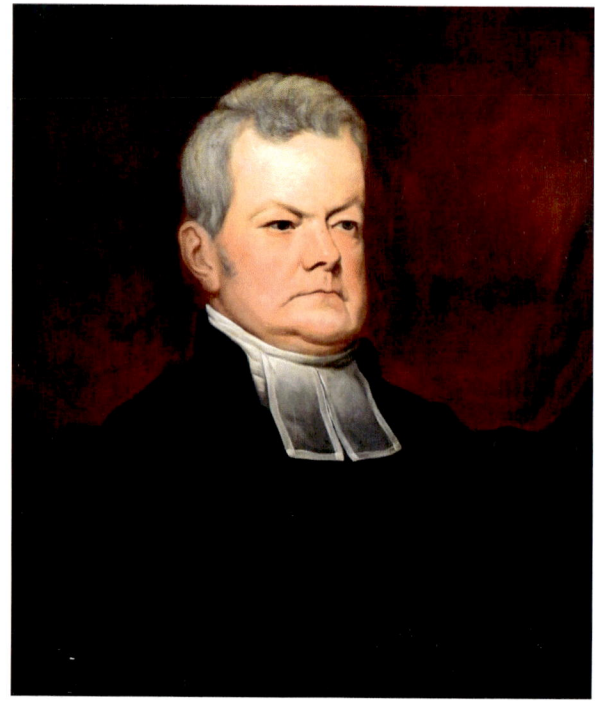

Left: Alexander Brodie.

Below: The Gore.

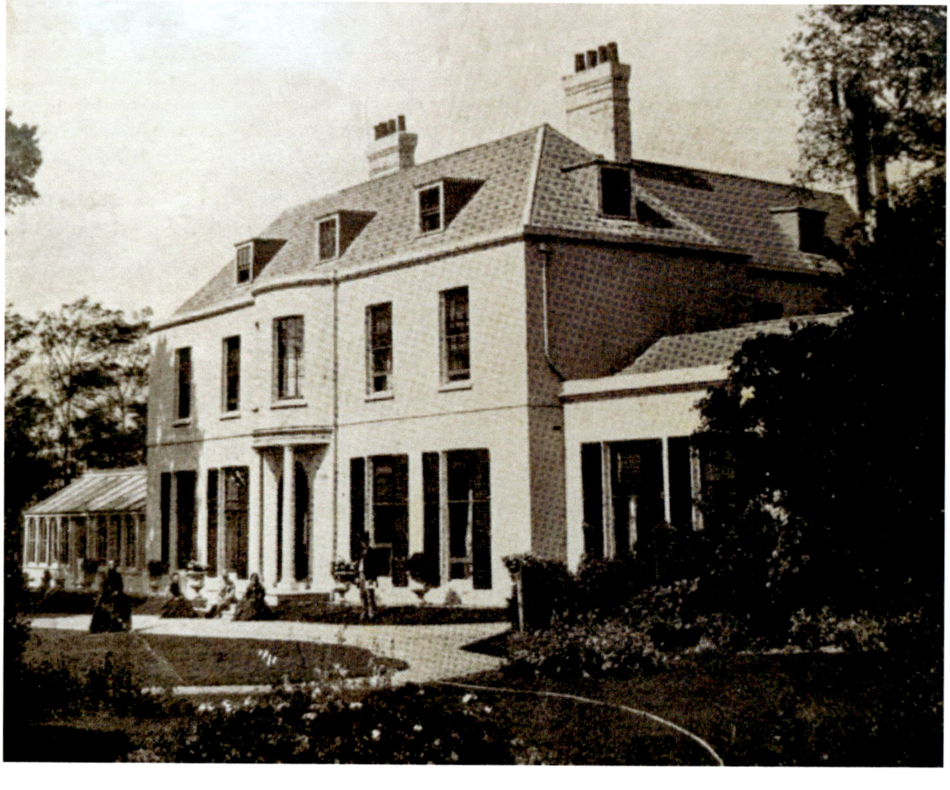

The Gore is described as 'A large mansion house, with 11 bedrooms, laundry, coach house, stables, outbuildings, lawn, pleasure grounds, extensive walled-in gardens well stocked with fruit trees. It included two pastures and five acres of land with extensive views of the sea and the Downs.' It was accessed from a drive that led from Ocklynge Road. The word 'gore' is an ancient name meaning a triangular or odd-shaped piece of land. There was a white boarded observatory which once stood in the grounds of the house and, for three weeks, during a particularly harsh winter in 1849 an igloo was actually built in the garden and was so substantial that tea was served in it!

In 1823, Anna, fell foul of the great English radical William Cobbett (1763–1835). Cobbett, famous for his book *Rural Rides* was a critic of corrupt governments and stood up for Catholics and the poor, especially the rural poor. He was a thorn in the side of the then Tory government.

Cobbett was clearly angry that, although Anna was a proprietor of *The Times* newspaper, which he believed was slandering him, she could hide behind the fact that she was a (vicar's) wife and had no responsibilities in law. Writing in his own newspaper *The Weekly Political Register*, Cobbett was brutal in his attacks on Anna calling her a she-bully, a blackguard and a foul-tongued streetwalker. He also accused her husband 'The Reverend Alexander Brodie of Eastbourne' of swaggering around London 'wearing a fire-shovel' hat!' (I believe that the Brodies

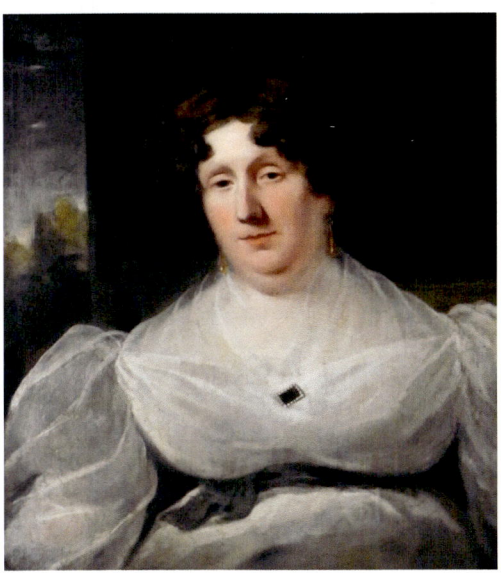 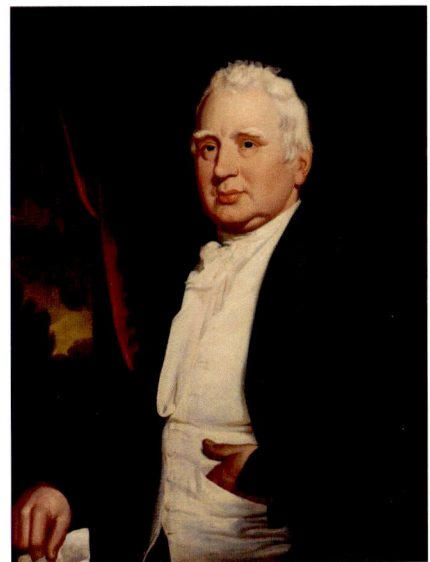

Above left: Mrs Anna Brodie.

Above right: William Cobbett.

owned property near the Strand in London – a fire-shovel hat was a tricorn hat with a long front traditionally worn by Anglican clergy. It was usually made of black beaver skin.)

Anna tried to win Cobbett over by the use of wit and poetry. In April 1828 he wrote an open letter to 'Anna Brodie, Wife of Doctor Brodie of Eastbourne in Sussex and principal owner of the *Old Times* newspaper'. Saying that he forgave her and in his admiring eyes she was now 'as clean and white as a smock from a washing-tub' and that she was indeed 'The Queen of the Press'. This may have been sarcastic though as the truce did not last and in 1833 Cobbett took her to court when *The Times* hinted that Cobbett was bankrupt. Anna had to pay Cobbett £100 damages for defamation, much less than the £5,000 he demanded, probably because of the insults that he himself had previously printed. Anna was clearly an influential person and a few weeks later there were demands for her to appear at the bar of the House of Commons to explain why *The Times* had printed details of a debate when only Hansard was allowed to do this.

Anna was a supporter of and probably friends with William Huskisson and George Canning. Huskisson (1770–1830) was the MP for Morpeth and is noted for being the first person to be killed by a railway train. Despite having a Northumbrian constituency he lived near Chichester and holidayed in nearby Seaford more than once. Canning (1770–1827) was Prime Minister and MP for Seaford and in September 1821 the two men and their families holidayed together in the town and it is more than likely that they would have visited their valued supporter Anna Brodie at the Gore just a few miles away in Eastbourne.

Before you leave take a look at the large Lushington Memorial on the south wall – it's the one with a bust of Henry Lushington (1738–63) who, despite being killed at the age of twenty-five years, had a full and adventurous life details of which can be read on his memorial. The young Henry was murdered and thrown down a well by 'Someroo', who was actually a German mercenary by the name of Walter Reinhardt. This is not the original site for the memorial – it was once hidden behind the church organ but was moved and placed here by Mr Lacy William Ridge (1840–1922). He was the church architect who was responsible for renovations of many Sussex churches including nearby Alfriston church.

Leave the church via the north door and you will emerge into the War Memorial Corridor that links the church to the Old Parsonage.

The Old Parsonage is a Tudor building which was later converted into three houses, each with its own fireplace and chimney. Despite its name, the building did not pass into church hands until 1912 when it was given to the parish by the Duke of Devonshire and restoration work started. Funds were not forthcoming to complete the work until 1924. Money was then donated by Amy Grant-Dalton of Ellerthwaite, a large house in The Goffs, in remembrance of her son Harold Grant-Dalton MC. Harold was a sub-lieutenant in the Royal Naval Volunteer Reserve. He was a member of 'The Hood Battalion', sailors that saw action on land, and in 1917 had received the Military Cross for gallantry. In March 1917 he was shot in the pelvis and could not get back to Allied lines. He was found by German soldiers and taken prisoner of war. He later died of his wounds in a German war hospital. The building now acts as a Vestry Hall and is occasionally open for coffee mornings and fetes.

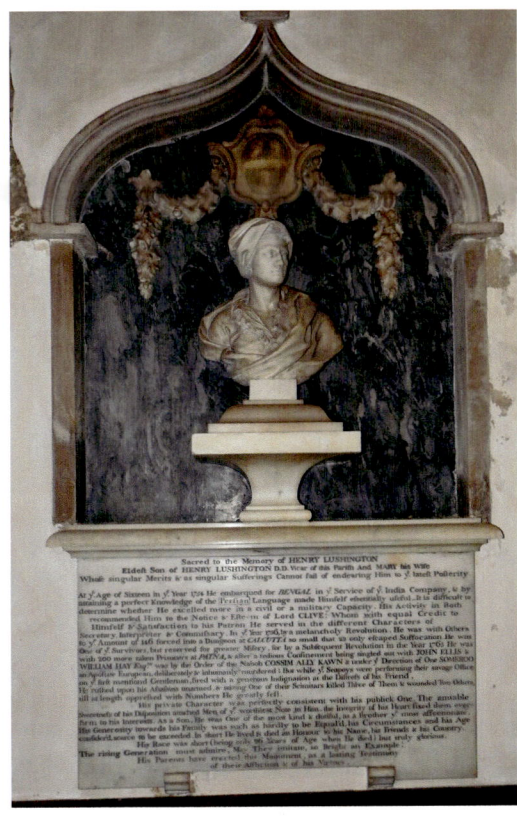

Right: Henry Lushington memorial.

Below: The Old Parsonage.

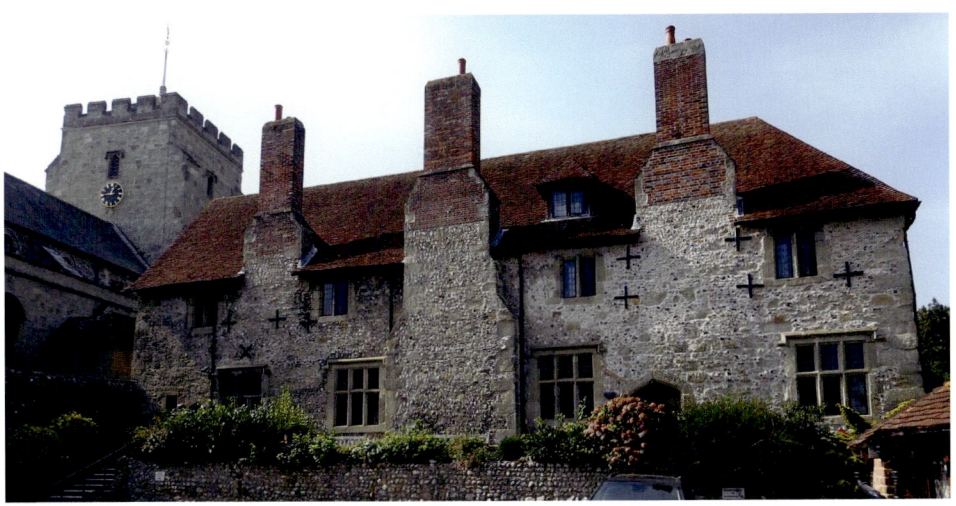

Devonshire Park

'The amusements of Eastbourne maybe summarised as Devonshire Park with a small et etcetera'. It is to Eastbourne, what Kurhaus is to Hamburg or the Casino is to Trouville and many visitors spend the greater part of the day there. Lawn Tennis is the game par-excellence at Devonshire Park and some of the best players in England are to be seen there. There is a cricket club, racquet court and cycling track, indeed everything that can be wished for by the most ardent follower of outdoor games.'

The Gentlewoman, April 1896

Today the Devonshire Quarter is hailed as the cultural heart of Eastbourne and consists of two theatres, an art gallery, an exhibition area, tourist centre, café and

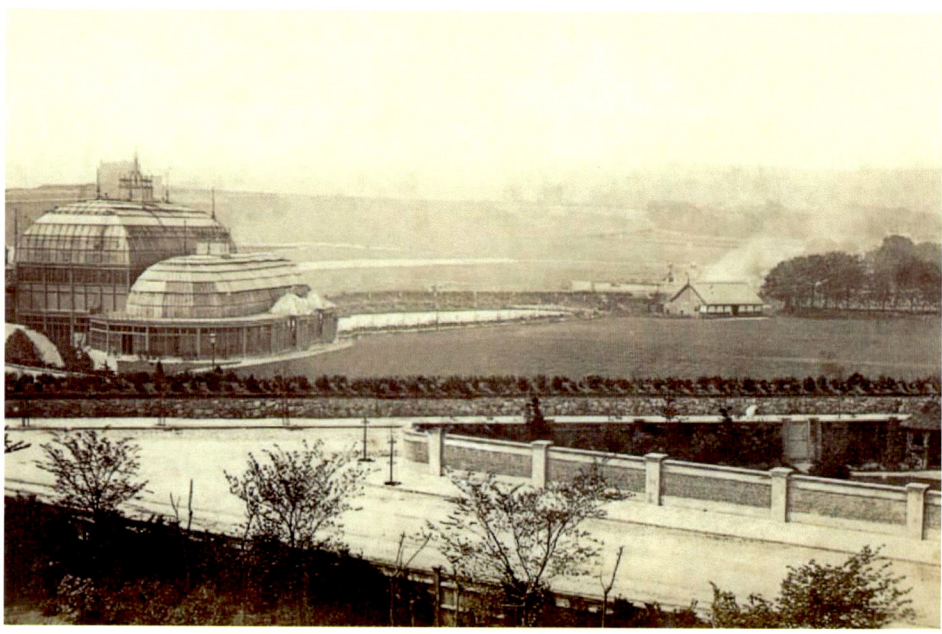

An early view of the park.

Devonshire Park, the home of international tennis. In 2024 the park celebrates its 150th anniversary.

Devonshire Park stands on a field previously used as a cricket ground. When the Duke of Devonshire established his new park, an alternative cricket ground was provided (close to what is now Tideswell Road) but it was never popular and local author George Chambers, writing in 1910, said that because of this, initially Devonshire Park gained little sympathetic support from the people of Eastbourne.

Devonshire Baths

The first attraction opened was a large swimming baths – 'The *Devonshire Baths*' of course. It was opened in April 1874 in Carlisle Road and here you could take a hot bath, cold bath, tepid bath, douche bath, shower bath, Turkish bath, hydropathic bath, vapour bath, seawater bath or freshwater bath. I hadn't realised there were so many different types of bath!. The gentlemen's pool was described as 'a delightful pond over 160 feet long and 30 feet broad varying in depth from four to six and a half feet surrounded by seventy dressing rooms'. These obviously impressed the *Eastbourne Gazette* who reported that there was 'no more picking the way over a pebbly beach like a cat on hot bricks.' Devonshire Baths claimed to be one of the largest baths in the kingdom and the largest tepid bath in the world. Like sea-swimming, there was to be no mixed bathing here – another, smaller, pool was 'dedicated for the use of ladies' but there was a fixed price for all – one shilling.

At high tide, seawater was pumped from near the Wish Tower, along a pipe into the baths. For the warm baths the water heated to 68°C. The large pump-house chimney was disguised by a grand Italianate style tower, which graced the area for many years – indeed as the pools were accessed down a long flight of stairs this was the only evidence of the grand swimming complex.

To encourage female swimmers, Sussex born Laura Saigeman was employed to give swimming displays in the ladies pool. According to the *Eastbourne Chronicle* Laura could swim 'backwards, forwards, sideways and flatways. She can waltz, dive and turn summersaults, imitate a dog and the seal and swim with her hands and feet tied as well as a host of other extraordinary feats'. In 1879 she had beaten her great rival Agnes Beckwith over three races and after this took the title 'Champion Lady Swimmer of England'. As Agnes also claimed to be the champion of the world Laura also assumed that title too!

On 31 October 1883 Laura took part in a 1-mile swimming race against Theresa Johnson for a £200 prize at the baths. The swim of thirty-three lengths was refereed by the editor of the *Sporting Life* and attracted a huge crowd. To considerable disappointment Eastbourne people, Laura lost by a minute and therefore lost her 'World Champion' title.

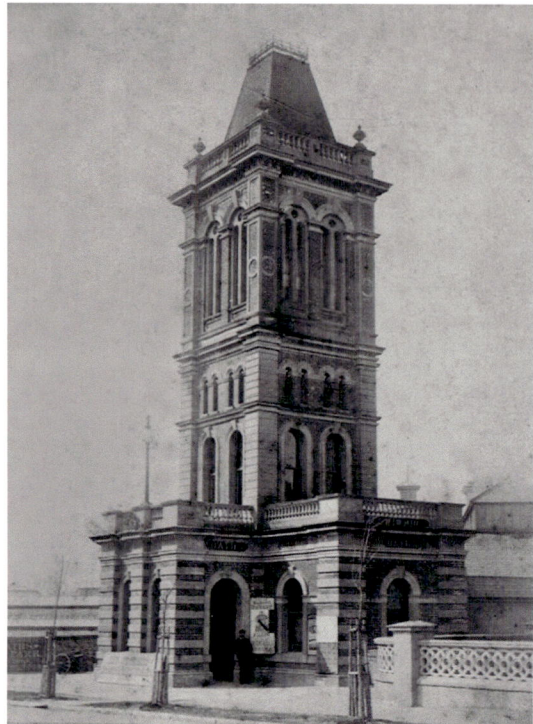

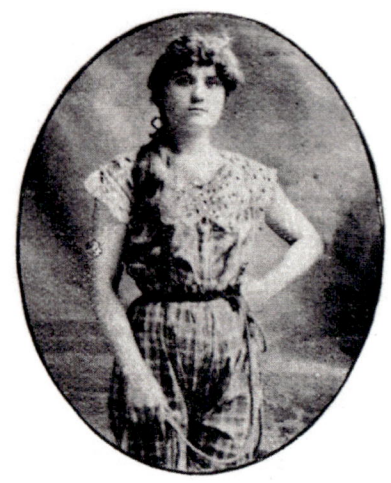

Above: Laura Saigeman.

Left: Entrance to Devonshire Baths.

Laura later became the 'Ladies Swimming Mistress' and in 1884 became the joint manager of the pool with her husband. They remained in Eastbourne until 1900 when Laura moved to Hastings to start a bathing machine business. She later moved back to Eastbourne and lived in Parsonage Road.

Devonshire Park

The nearby 11 acres of Devonshire Park were opened to the public without ceremony on Wednesday 1 July 1874. At this time there were few facilities, the trees and plants were freshly planted and there was a lack of seating and not too much to do. The local press, however, was optimistic saying that a skating rink was planned and new cricket, badminton and croquet clubs were being established. Also, 'the game of tennis will be provided'. Maybe, because of earlier criticism, a cricket club was soon established and, on 11 July, the Devonshire Park Cricket Club played Eastbourne College on the newly laid turf. Diplomatically the game was declared to be a draw.

One of the first events at the new park was the Eastbourne Flower Show, which was held on 27 and 28 August 1874. This was not a quiet event, as the 'exhibition of flowers and fruits' was accompanied by the Band of the Coldstream Guards! Flower Shows were very popular in the early years of the park; in November 1884

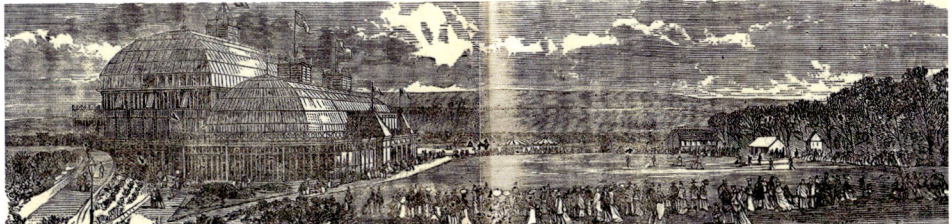

A cricket match at Devonshire Park.

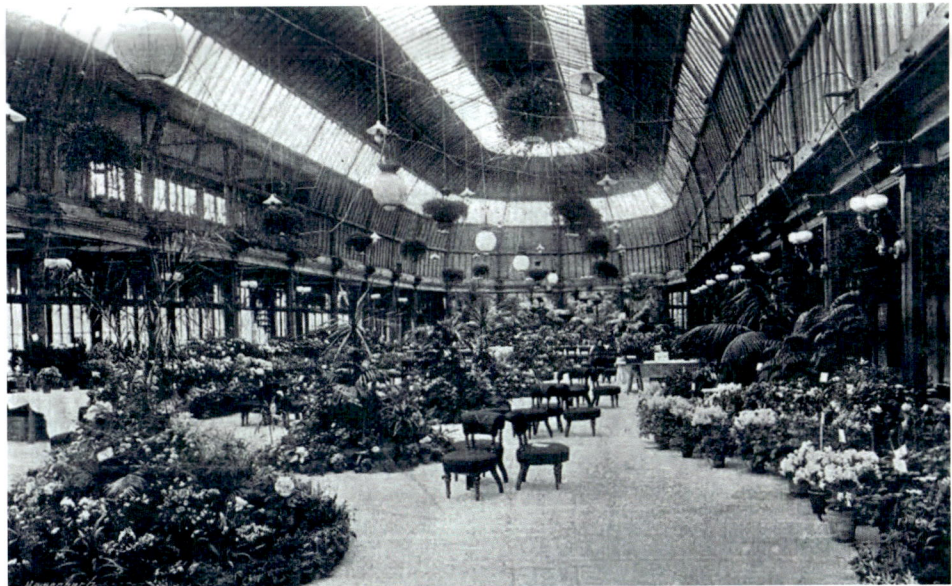

The Floral Hall.

there was a Grand Exhibition of Chrysanthemums in the aptly named Floral Hall boasting over 3,000 chrysanthemums in 300 varieties.

The year 1874 saw proposals for a roller-skating rink, an aquarium and Winter Gardens. The aquarium did not materialise but the Winter Garden and nearby skating rink were constructed in 1875. The 1,558-yard asphalt roller-skating rink was opened on the anniversary of the park's opening at 4.30 p.m. on 1 July 1875. Despite it being a rainy day, over 200 people watched displays of skating by Mr Plimpton and his family, who danced a quadrille and 'achieved wonderful ornamental movements'. James Leonard Plimpton (1828–1911) was the American inventor of the modern four-wheel roller skate and was president of the New York Skating Association (the world's first roller skating club). He had patented his roller skate in 1863 and his endorsement was quite a coup for Devonshire Park.

The roller-skating rink was lined with white asphalt to imitate ice and a band was often present to accompany the skaters. The rink was popular, probably because (unlike the nearby swimming pool) both sexes could participate in the

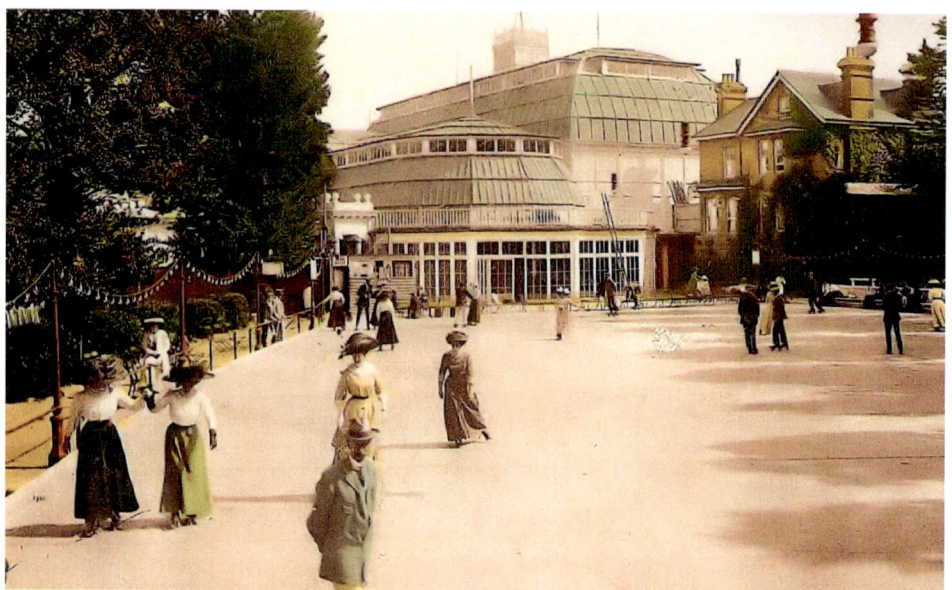

Roller skating at Devonshire Park.

new sport of 'rinking' together. It was said that the rink could accommodate 500 skaters but it is unlikely that it was ever that busy, although in 1909 there was a 'Roller Skating Carnival' with over 100 skaters. The *Eastbourne Gazette* said 'Youths find roller-skating one of their chief occupations and think of nothing else. There is a new catch phrase: "Do you roll?"'

The nearby Winter Garden was basically an elegant large conservatory with flower beds and vines creeping up its cast-iron columns. It was also used as a concert hall and exhibition space and initially the large French windows could be thrown open to allow skaters to glide in and out. The building had a stage and reading and smoking rooms. It was clearly an excellent venue for those (rare) days when the Eastbourne sun did not shine.

The 'New Concert Room' in the Winter Garden was also known as 'The Pavilion' and hosted its first concert on Saturday 8 July 1876. The star act was Madame Edith Wynne, a Welsh singer hailed as 'The best vocalist in the country' but a few hours before the start of the concert she sent Devonshire Park a telegram to say she was too ill to make the journey to Eastbourne. Madame Blanche Cole, a twenty-five-year-old opera singer, stepped in and was a great success.

She was first in a long list of musicians and entertainers to take the stage at Devonshire Park. The following year it hosted a variety of entertainments including Herr Adalbert Frikell, 'The famous German Professor of Physical and Natural Mystery presenting Extraordinary fantastical manipulations of ancient and modern miracles and marvellous metamorphoses', Miss Grace Armytage with her Burlesque Company, The Royal Osborne Hand-bell Ringers, Professor

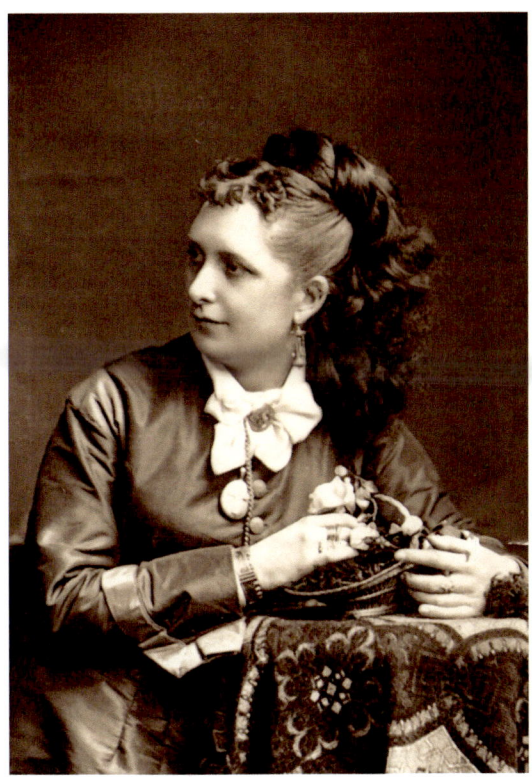

Right: Blanche Cole.

Below: The Winter Garden.

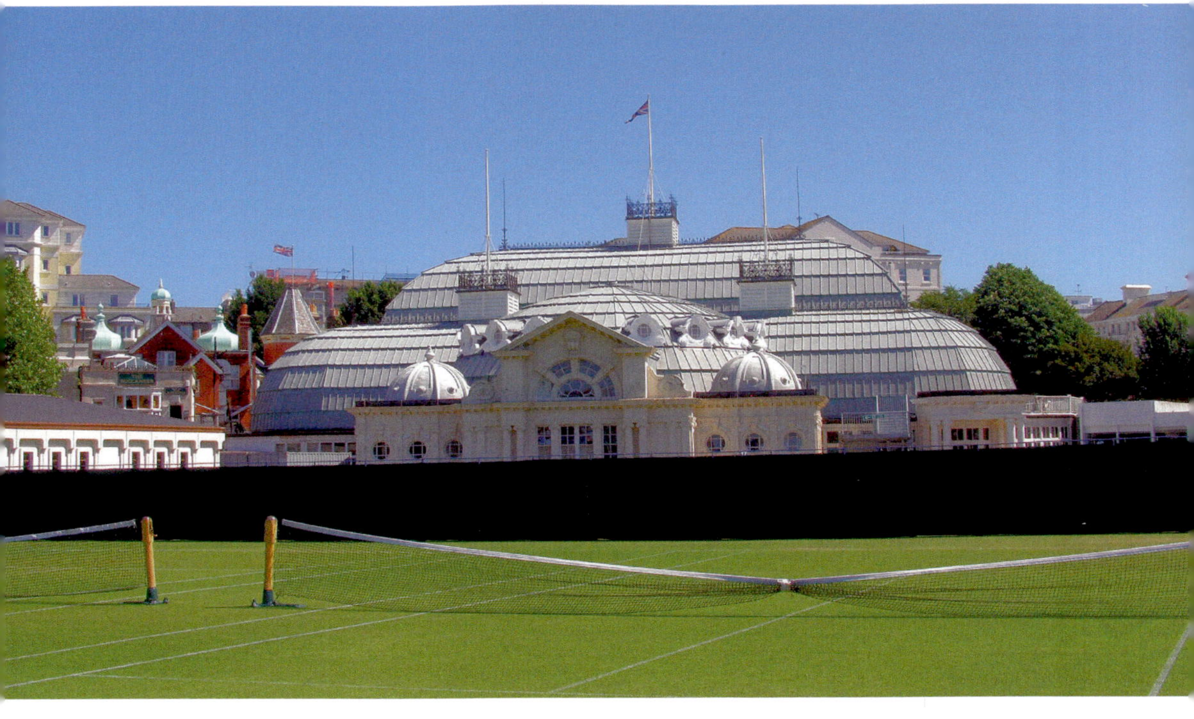

Pepper and his Grand Science Festival and 'A Grand Assault-at Arms by the 20th Hussars.'

The Pavilion was used as a theatre, concert hall, venue for fundraising bazaars and a lecture hall. In November 1883, Oscar Wilde delivered a lecture here on 'Personal Impressions of America'.

The Duke of Devonshire's Park seemed to have all that was needed for all-round entertainment but yet another building was needed – a theatre – and the duke's favourite architect Henry Currey (1820–1900) was commissioned to design it. Currey had trained under the great architect Decimus Burton, who in the 1830s had designed Eastbourne's Holy Trinity Church. Currey had designed St Thomas' Hospital on the banks of the River Thames (to a design approved by Florence Nightingale) and the grand 250-room hotel at London Bridge station.

The 1880s had seen a number of serious fires in theatres which had led to the deaths of hundreds of people. In 1878, a German engineer, August Foelsh, published a paper about fires in theatres. In the previous century no less than

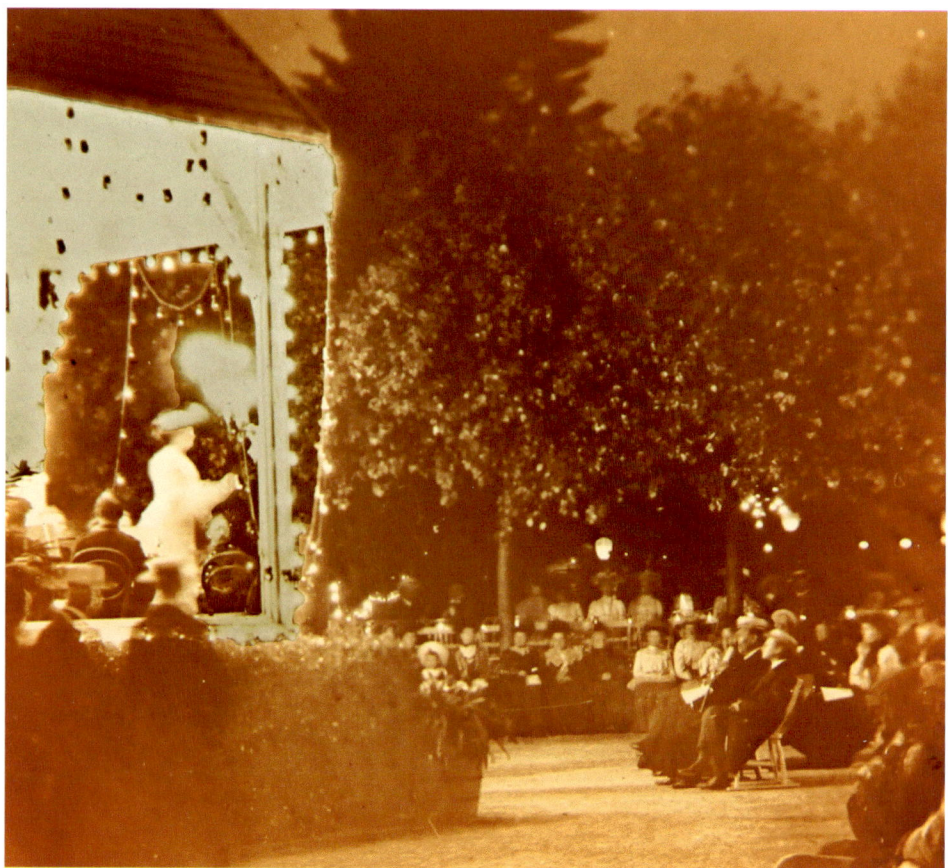

An open-air concert at Devonshire Park.

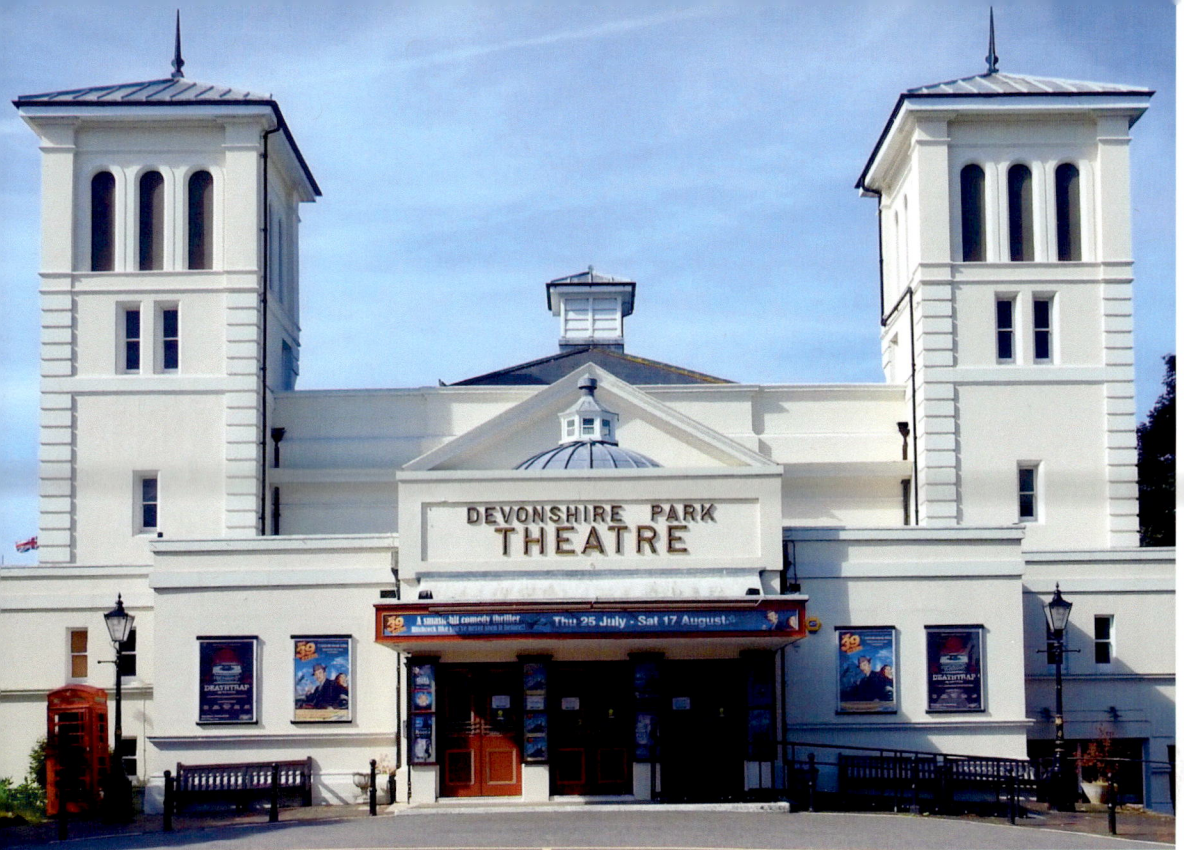

Devonshire Park Theatre.

460 theatres worldwide had burnt down, thirty-one of them in London. At this time theatres were lit by gas and the stages were illuminated by spluttering limelight (a naked flame directed onto a piece of quicklime). There were few 'health and safety' concerns and once a performance started all the doors were often locked. It is clear that Currey designed the new Devonshire Park Theatre with these facts in mind. On either side of the entrance there are two large Italianate style towers, which were fireproofed and housed massive water tanks attached to hydrants. The towers each contained 'incombustible emergency staircases' and Currey's new theatre also included 'four emergency exits'. The theatre was not only splendid but safe. The outside of the building belies the magnificent interior. *The Stage* reported that 'Mr Currey has not taxed his skills upon the external structure but has devoted himself to making the interior as near perfection as possible'. The colour scheme was buff and gold and Maples of Tottenham Court Road, London, provided the upholstery, carpets and curtains. London artist Albert Callcott painted a large depiction of Herstmonceux Castle as the act-drop – the curtain that drops between scenes.

Just before the theatre opened Mr Alfred Standen Triggs was appointed not only as director of the new theatre but the whole of Devonshire Park. He was introduced to the audience at the first performance on Monday 2 June 1884. The play was *The Day After the Wedding* performed by the Garrick Comedy

Company and afterwards the leading actor George M. Wood addressed the audience in rhyme:

> Eastbourne – Empress of the South!
> To sound her praise I must open my mouth
> Her boulevards are even a Frenchman's joy
> I hear him say 'Mon dieu, je suis chez moi'
>
> Her shady trees the German's heart must win, then
> Recalling happy days unter den Linden
> Improvements march so rapidly apace
> In Seaside 'Derby's' – Eastbourne wins the race!
>
> Obliging tradesmen, civil, not too dear
> Most visitors, I think experience here.
> Hotels, I don't know where you'll beat them
> And churches, at every step you meet them
>
> You are soon to have a new Town Hall
> Where justice holds the scales and mirth her ball
> Receptions worth of some Royal guest
> Or public meetings – rights or wrongs to test
>
> Eastbourne in Parliament must represented be
> And her first Mayor (Wallace) maybe her first MP
> In singing praise, I'll go one higher
> And name His Grace the Duke of Devonshire
>
> No prouder monument can tribute pay
> Than simply Eastbourne of today
> Parks, baths, pavilion and last not least
> This thespian fane, dramatic taste to feast
> If theatres you search from pole to pole
> You'll find not better on the whole!

He then called to the stage the architect Henry Currey and the new manager, Alfred Standen Triggs. Thirty-six-year-old Triggs was from Chichester where, as a fifteen-year-old, he had arranged 'lecture entertainments' at his school. The press said his manner was easy, natural and effective. Although a cotton trader by profession, Alfred was an experienced thespian and impresario and clearly just right for the job. He managed the theatre well and even appeared in several productions. Triggs soon became a member of the local (Hartington) Lodge of the Freemasons and seemed to be well respected by all.

Many esteemed performances were held at the new theatre. In August 1894, it was crowded with a 'fashionable audience' to watch *A Bunch of Violets*. Two seats in the front row were reserved for theatre royalty in the form of the great actor-manager Henry Irving and his favourite leading lady Ellen Terry.

Manager Alfred Triggs specialised in arranging 'flying matinees' when top acts from the West End came down to Eastbourne to appear on stage before taking the train back to London to appear on stage in the evening. A particular favourite was Lily Langtry. She would often hire a whole train to bring the complete cast of a play to Eastbourne for just one performance. This probably gives some indication of how much she was paid!

Another sellout was a lecture in November 1900 by the newly elected MP for Oldham – the twenty-six-year-old Winston Churchill. The event was so over-subscribed that Triggs set out chairs in the orchestra pit and even on the stage itself. Churchill's talk 'The War as I Saw It' was about his experiences during the Boer War. He was introduced by Lindsay Hogg, Eastbourne's MP, and the lecture was illustrated by large maps and lantern slides. The local press described Churchill as speaking with a lisp and being slightly built, ruddy with an abundance of hair – not how we remember Churchill today!

The lack of seating for Churchill's talk annoyed the manager and he persuaded the Devonshire Park Company to upgrade the theatre. Triggs wanted the best theatre designer and he managed to obtain the services of Francis (Frank) Matcham (1854–1920). At that time Matcham had just completed the contract

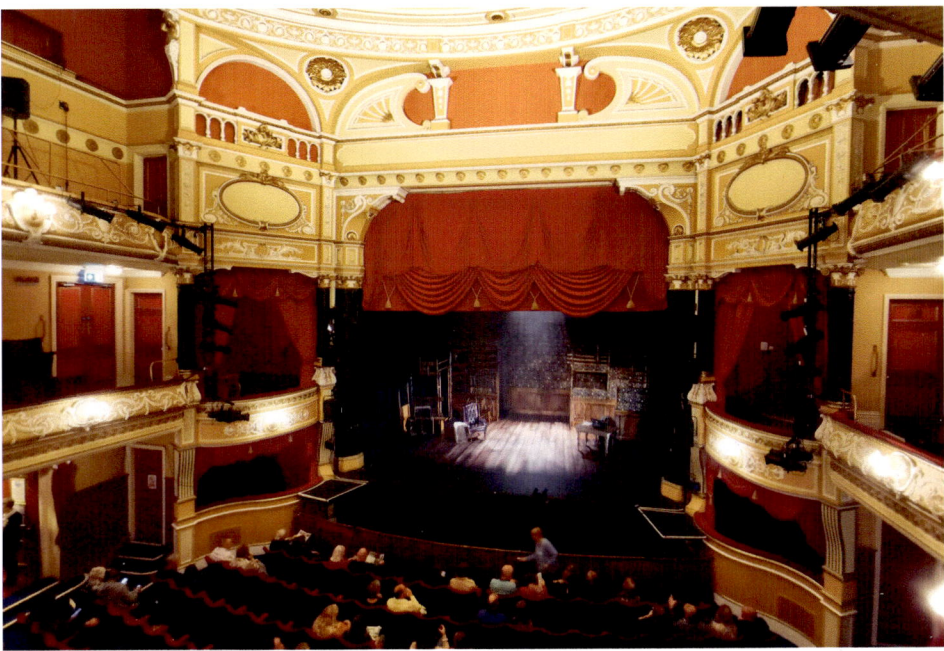

Devonshire Park Theatre (interior).

for designing the Hippodrome, Coliseum and Hackney Empire theatres in London. He was also responsible for the design of the famous Tower Ballroom at Blackpool. A local builder, Joe Martin, was chosen to do the work.

Although the original façade with its two tall 'fire-towers' was retained, the rest of the theatre was transformed into the wonderful theatre we still cherish today. Patrons marvelled at the decoration and the well-upholstered tip-up seats. Although there were more seats, there were better views of the stage and the building was lit with 'a festoon of electric lamps in opulent globes' the *Eastbourne Gazette* described it as 'one of the handsomest, best ventilated and most comfortable playhouses in England'.

The whole reconstruction had taken just three months and Mr Triggs, the manager, again was able to get a world-class actress for the reopening on Friday 31 July 1903. Mrs Patrick Campbell reprised her greatest role in the play *The Second Mrs Tanqueray* in the presence of a 'large and brilliant audience'. The *Eastbourne Gazette* enthused that Mrs Pat (as she was known) was 'one of the greatest actresses of this or any other age' and reported that 'the gentlemen in the audience wore evening dress and the toilettes of the ladies set off their charms to the greatest advantage'. It was clear that the newly reopened theatre was a place to see and be seen – all lit by the 'new and welcome multitudinous electric lights'.

Today the Devonshire Park Theatre is still a joy to visit. The nearby Congress Theatre (opened in 1965) may be modern and much larger but the Devonshire Park Theatre is still welcoming, with its old-fashioned comfort and spectacular interior decoration.

The Indian Pavilion

The Royal Naval Exhibition was staged at Chelsea during the summer of 1891. There were several temporary buildings and one of them, the Peninsular and Oriental Pavilion, was purchased by the Duke of Devonshire to be re-erected in Devonshire Park in the following year. It was known as the Indian Pavilion.

For many years it hosted grand balls and dinners. The Pavilion could be hired out for meetings, exhibitions and entertainments. I was amused to read that in July 1894 the Pavilion hosted Mazeppa, who could understand English, German and French. Mazeppa could tell the time and do complex calculations – given a person's age he could calculate the year of their birth. If you are not impressed, Mazeppa was a horse!

In 1958 the name of the Pavilion was changed to the Devonshire Lawns Restaurant. But the change of name did not improve its popularity and it was demolished to make way for the Congress Theatre in 1963.

Alfred Standen Triggs was clearly an innovative manager, not only of the theatre but the whole of Devonshire Park. On 12 October 1897 a balloon voyage

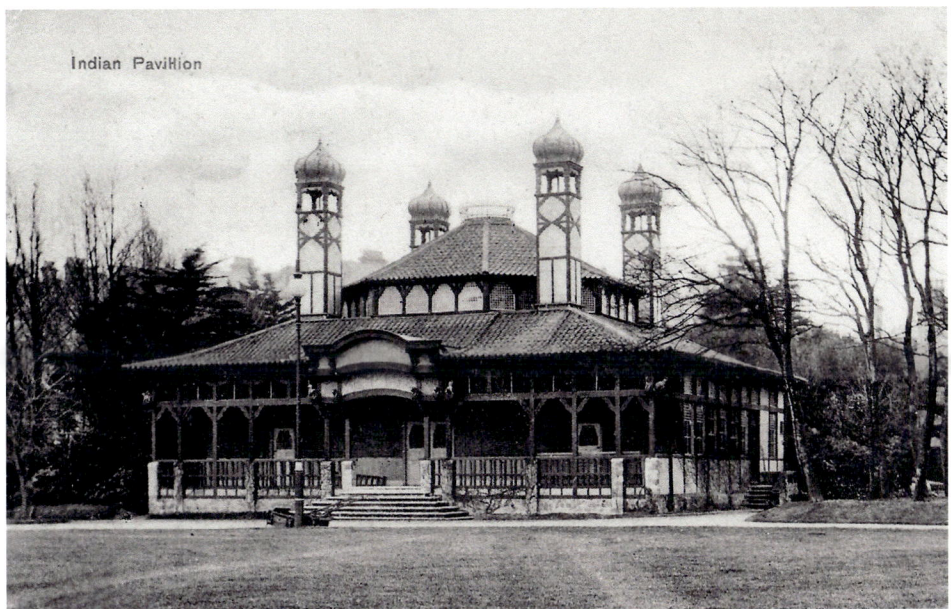

Indian Pavilion

The Indian Pavilion.

to France started from Devonshire Park (the Eastbourne Gas Company were in readiness to help should extra fuel be needed). He was to remain as the manager of the Devonshire Park estate until his retirement in 1906 but was remembered for many years afterwards. In May 1950 the *Eastbourne Herald* exclaimed: 'As we watch the Davis Cup we think of the late pioneer Mr Standen Triggs, who would be surprised to know that tennis matches on his Devonshire Park courts are now broadcast around the world!'

As we have heard, Devonshire Park was a venue for sports from the very beginning when it first opened in 1874. Within two years croquet lawns, badminton courts and bowling greens were laid out near to the cricket ground. Sport was becoming more popular especially with women and Eastbourne had three bicycling clubs, all of which met at Devonshire Park. The Devonshire Park Cycling Academy offered 'lessons to ladies visiting Eastbourne who are desirous to acquire the necessary art of wheeling in the correct style'.

The games of tennis and croquet were linked by needing a well-cut lawn, which was not possible until the invention of the lawnmower in mid-nineteenth century. Croquet was first played in the 1850s and was particularly popular as it was one of the few games that allowed men and women to play on equal terms. The first croquet club in the country opened in Worthing in 1860, the rules were codified in 1864 and the All-England Croquet Club was established at Wimbledon in 1868. In 1896 the sport entered a new era with new rules, smaller hoops and larger mallets. Tournaments were established and that same year Mr Standen Triggs announced a Grand Open Croquet Tournament to be held at Devonshire Park

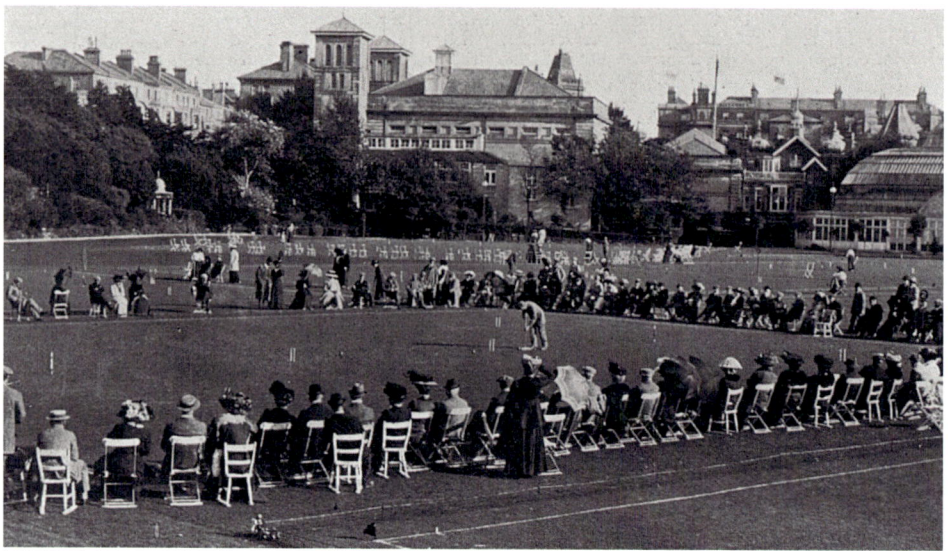

Croquet at Devonshire Park.

for the week commencing 21 September. Two years later the Eastbourne Croquet Club was established.

A local reporter 'Invictus' reported how exciting the new game was saying that if only an element of danger could be introduced the game would be as popular as football. He said that 'Croquet was something like horse-racing – the idea being to get over the course as fast as you can while at the same time preventing your opponent by fair means or foul from getting in front of you.' The game was so popular at this time that it even featured in the 1900 Olympic Games – indeed croquet was the very first game played by women at the Olympics. Two years later no less than 502 players took part in a croquet tournament at Devonshire Park and by 1904 croquet was so popular that it ousted cricket. Mr Standen Triggs announced 'It is not without regret that in view of the growth and increasing demands of modern croquet, the management of Devonshire Park have decided to omit cricket for the present season.' Cricket moved to The Saffrons where it had been played for many years and never returned to Devonshire Park.

The 1904 Eastbourne Croquet Tournament was 'watched with much interest by a large and fashionable company'. The *Gentlewoman* newspaper reported that the Eastbourne Tournament was 'always the most popular fixture of the year and a great many well-known players make an effort to be present'.

By now the Eastbourne Tournament was so popular it was being covered by the national press. Photographs showed the winning ladies in huge dresses and equally large floral hats.

The South of England Croquet Championships were held at Devonshire Park from 1904 until the early 1980s when they moved to Compton Croquet Club

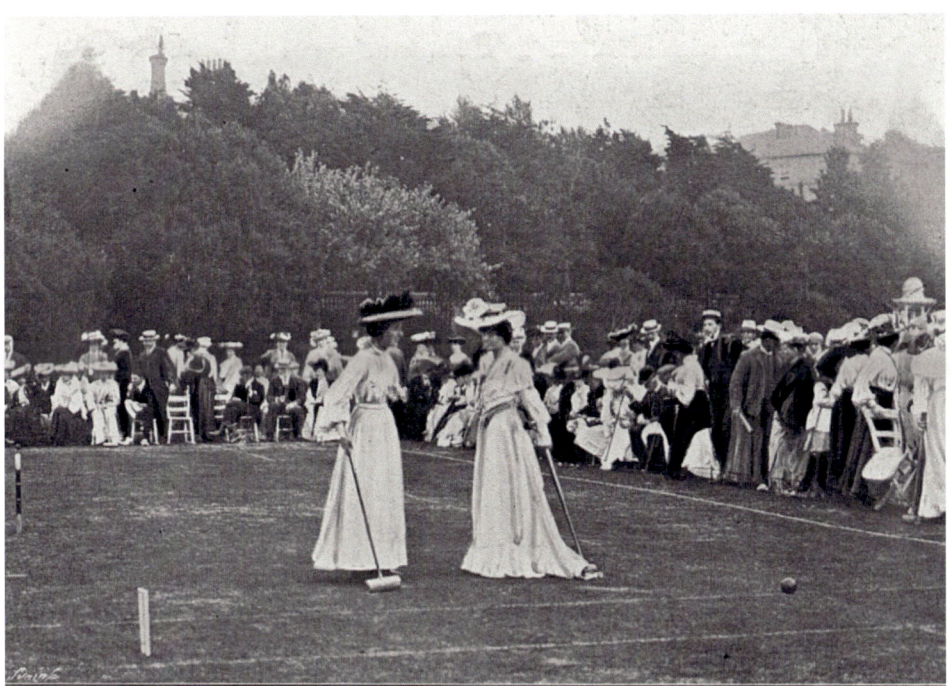

The Open Croquet Tournament at Devonshire Park, Eastbourne.—Miss N. E. Coote and Miss Gower, after their game in the Open Singles.

Above and below: 1904 Croquet Tournament winners.

NAVY AND ARMY.　　　THE KING.　　　Oct. 15th, 1904.

THE CROQUET TOURNAMENT AT EASTBOURNE.

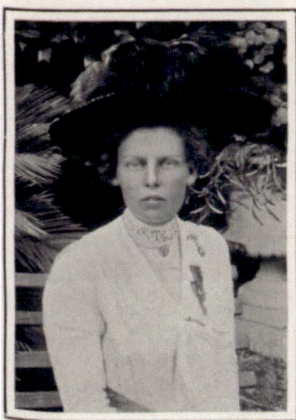

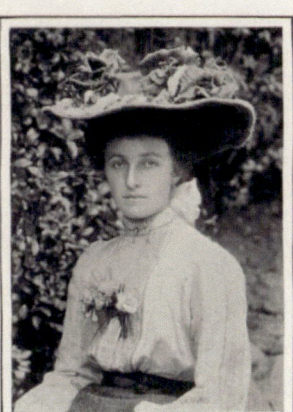

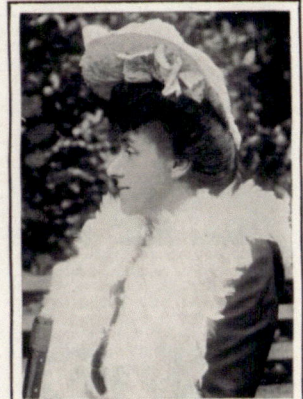

MISS GOWER.
Champion Lady croquet player.

MISS COOTE.
Winner of the tournament.

MISS M. AVERAY JONES.
One of the semi-final winners.

at The Saffrons. In 1959 the tournament was covered by the *Tatler* magazine, who stated that the game was 'gaining ground amongst young intellectuals'. By this time Lawn Tennis had become the principal sport at Devonshire Park, with croquet occupying just two weeks at the end of the season.

Apart from back gardens, croquet was first played in Eastbourne on a field off Ashford Road near the railway station. A two-day tournament was held here in September 1869. The patrons were the Duke of Devonshire and his sister, Lady Fanny Howard of Compton Place.

The Compton Croquet Club was established in April 1898 by Swedish born doctor Otto Holst, who lived at No. 20 Upperton Gardens. Fifteen people were present at the inaugural meeting of which only four were men.

Today the Club has five full-sized lawns and a clubhouse at The Saffrons ground and a membership of over 100. Some of the Eastbourne players are on their way to becoming among the top players in the country and in August 2024 the club will host the European Women's Championships.

Compton Croquet Club today. (Compton Croquet Club)

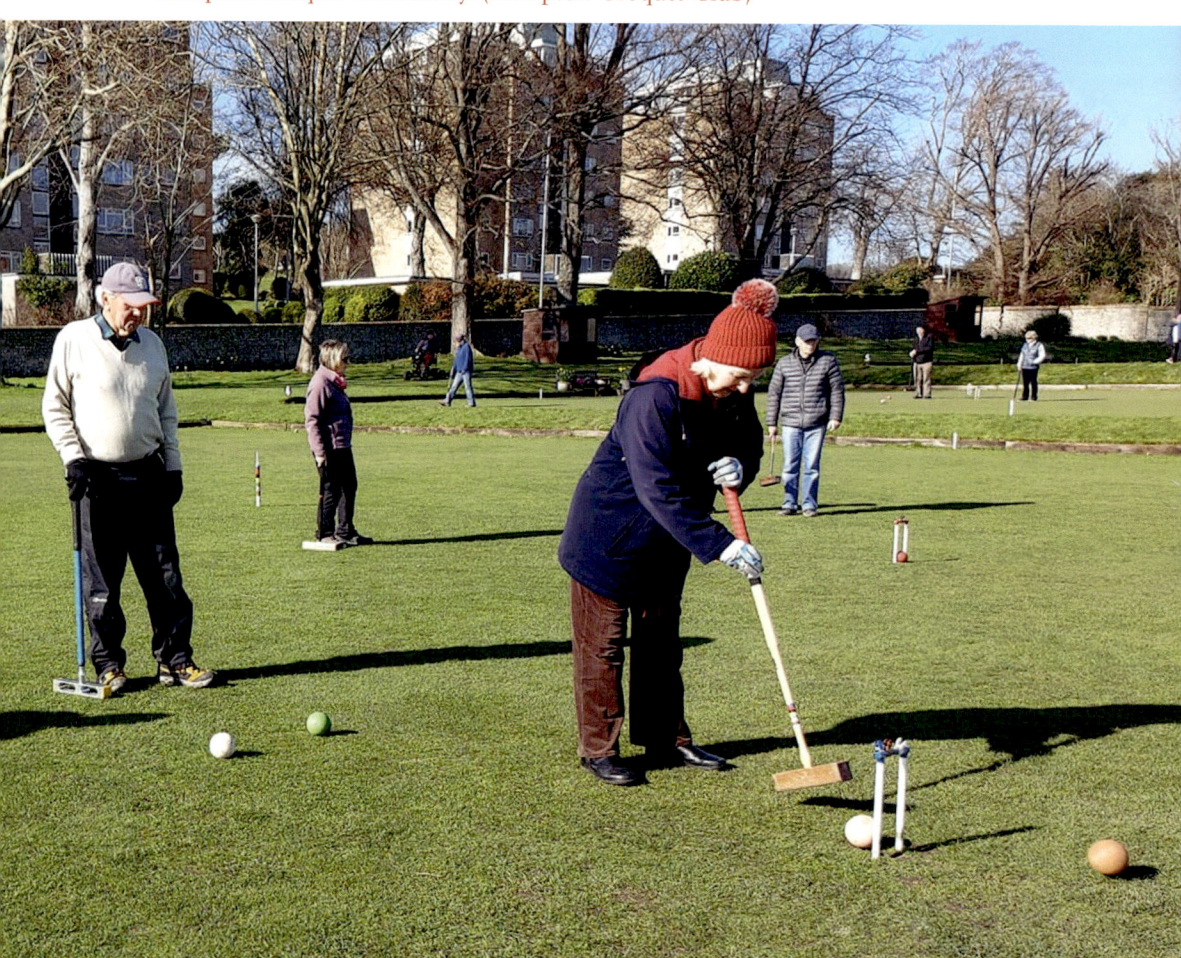

It is interesting that it is often reported that competitions at Devonshire Park attracted a 'fashionable crowd' and this seems to suggest that 'ordinary' Eastbournians were excluded. This seems to be evidenced by the *Eastbourne Gazette* of 14 September 1881, who seemed to defend this stance: 'It has been urged against Devonshire Park that its prices preclude the general public from participating in its advantages but it must be remembered that the Park has amongst its chief patrons people who can well afford and are satisfied to pay prices of admission and these are the very people who, by their stay in Eastbourne benefit the town in a financial way.'

Tennis

Tennis has been around for centuries but in 1874 Major Walter Wingfield, one-time royal bodyguard and director of the Alcazar Theatre in London, published a pamphlet entitled 'Sphairistrike or Lawn Tennis', which outlined the modern game we know today, albeit it was played on an hourglass-shaped court. The *Contemporary Review* of April 1878 said that in inventing the game Wingfield had 'done more for the health of women of this country than 10,000 doctors'.

When Major Wingfield retired in 1881 the *Eastbourne Chronicle* urged its readers to subscribe to his testimonial saying 'the health of the younger generation is down to lawn-tennis – it teaches a man to be a man and a woman to be helpful and energetic. It does not un-nerve a woman as cricket or boating would do, nor require more strength than would be considered womanly, but gives a grace of figure, a freeness of gait and an appearance of health which adds to a woman's attraction'. In July 1881 Major Wingfield himself chose Eastbourne as his holiday destination and I am sure he would have visited Devonshire Park to see his very own game being played!

Rules of tennis and the use of a rectangular court had been ratified by the All-England Lawn Tennis and Croquet Club at Wimbledon in 1875 and two years later the first tournament was held. The Wimbledon Tennis tournament is the oldest in the world. Eastbourne was not far behind as the first tournament held at Devonshire Park was between 15 and 22 August 1881. This was so successful that there were two further tournaments that year. These, however, were for men; the first ladies tournament was not held until 1885. The first prize was 7 guineas.

The first ladies champion at Eastbourne was twenty-three-year-old Blanche Bingley, a tailor's daughter and amateur dramatics enthusiast from West London. She was an up-and-coming player who was already the Ladies Champion of Middlesex. The previous year she participated in the first ever Wimbledon championship.

Amazingly the Eastbourne event was mainly covered in the local press as a fashion item! One player (maybe Blanche herself) was wearing a 'remarkably pretty cream flannel gown with full treble box-pleats and round scarf drapery'.

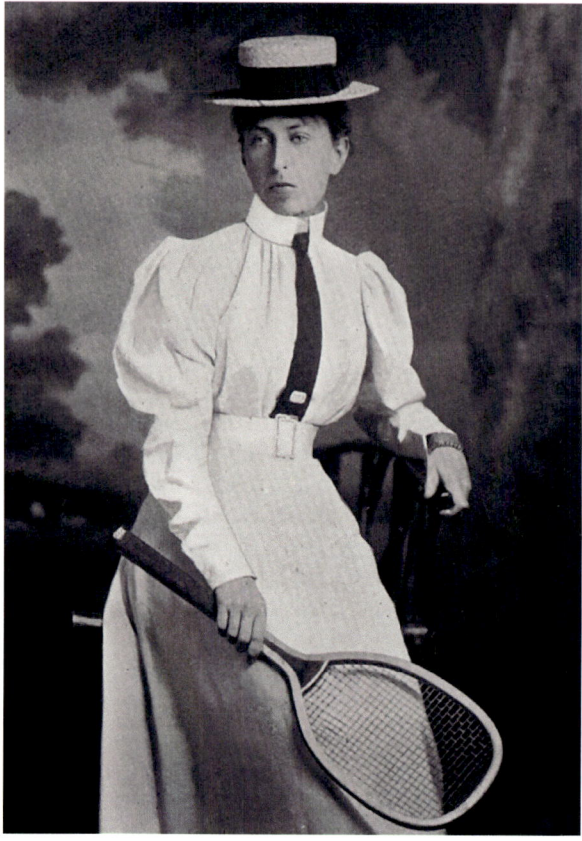

Blanche Bingley. (Wimbledon
Lawn Tennis Museum)

The skirt had seven lines of turquoise blue braid and the top had a high military
collar and pointed cuffs. The reporter said that the dress was very suitable for
tennis and was worn by 'a daughter of the gods, divinely tall and divinely fair'.
Women were not permitted to wear shorts for tennis at Devonshire Park until
1933. Blanche went on to play in no less than thirteen Wimbledon ladies singles
finals, winning on six occasions.

In 1900 Harvard University arranged a competition between British and
American tennis players. The first competition was held in Boston as the
International Lawn Tennis Challenge until one of the American players, Dwight
Davis, paid for a trophy, and subsequent competitions were known as The Davis
Cup. By 1910, other nations started to participate, making it a true international
competition. The first Davis Cup tournament to be played after the First World
War was held at Devonshire Park. The same year (1919) the first Professional
Lawn Tennis Championships of Great Britain were held at Eastbourne. Our town
was getting a reputation around the world as a centre for tennis.

The Davis Cup brought internationally famous tennis stars to Eastbourne
including Fred Perry, Bunny Austin and Rene Lacoste. Other competitions were
also held at the park including County and Youth Championships.

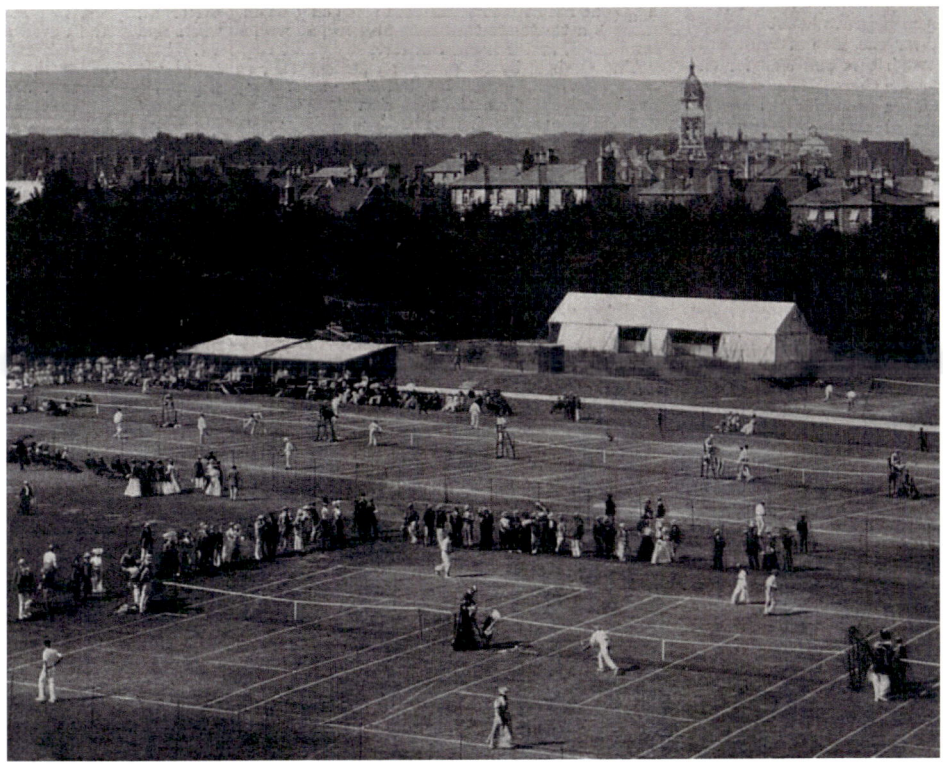

An early tennis championship at Devonshire Park.

Devonshire Park was clearly an important asset and in 1923 the council proposed that it should be purchased for the people of Eastbourne. In January 1924 the council listed all the park resources, which included not only the grounds, swimming baths and theatre but also a public house, two bandstands, a laundry, dwelling houses and several shops. The Duke of Devonshire agreed to sell the whole estate for £103,577 but it was agreed that the final say should be with the ratepayers. There was a poll on 25 January and although 1,822 people voted for the sale to go ahead, 6,312 voted against.

Devonshire Park was indeed later sold to the council but on a plot-by-plot basis: the Swimming Baths in 1924, the Winter Garden in 1930, the park in 1946 and the theatre in 1957.

The war years took their toll, not only on Devonshire Park but on the whole of the town, which was heavily bombed. The park became overgrown and its buildings forlorn and tatty. Beaches were covered with barbed wire defences and even the pier was cut in half should it be used during a German invasion.

Eastbourne Council needed to return the town to its pre-war status as 'Empress of the South' and entice back visitors. An investment was made by building a covered stand for the tennis courts and Devonshire Park started to lure some important tennis championships including the Inter-County Championships, the Professional Championship of Great Britain and in 1954 an International Exhibition Contest, which attracted players such as Dan Maskell, Fred Perry and Ken Rosewall. In 1957 the Slazenger Professional Lawn Tennis Tournament moved from Yorkshire to Eastbourne.

Prestigious tennis tournaments often only allowed either professional or amateur players to compete, but the 'Open Era' of tennis started in 1968 when the rules were relaxed to allow all-comers to compete together.

The 1,700-seat Congress Theatre was opened at Devonshire Park in 1973 and the British Travel and Holiday Association declared it was the best new tourist attraction that year. Men's tennis had always taken the lion's share of sponsorship and publicity but that same year Billie Jean King won a tennis match in the USA known as the 'Battle of the Sexes' when she beat former American champion Bobbie Riggs. This match was televised around the world and changed people's attitudes to female tennis.

Globally, four tennis competitions became the most famous – now known as the 'Grand Slam' venues. These were (are) the US Open, the Australian Open, the French Open and Wimbledon. The Australian and American venues are hard courts, the French tournament is played on clay and Wimbledon is still played on grass – and this fact is advantageous to Eastbourne! Prior to the Wimbledon Championships every June players need to practise on a good grass court. The men use the Queens Club in London as a 'Wimbledon warmup' and the women come to Eastbourne.

Devonshire Park tennis.

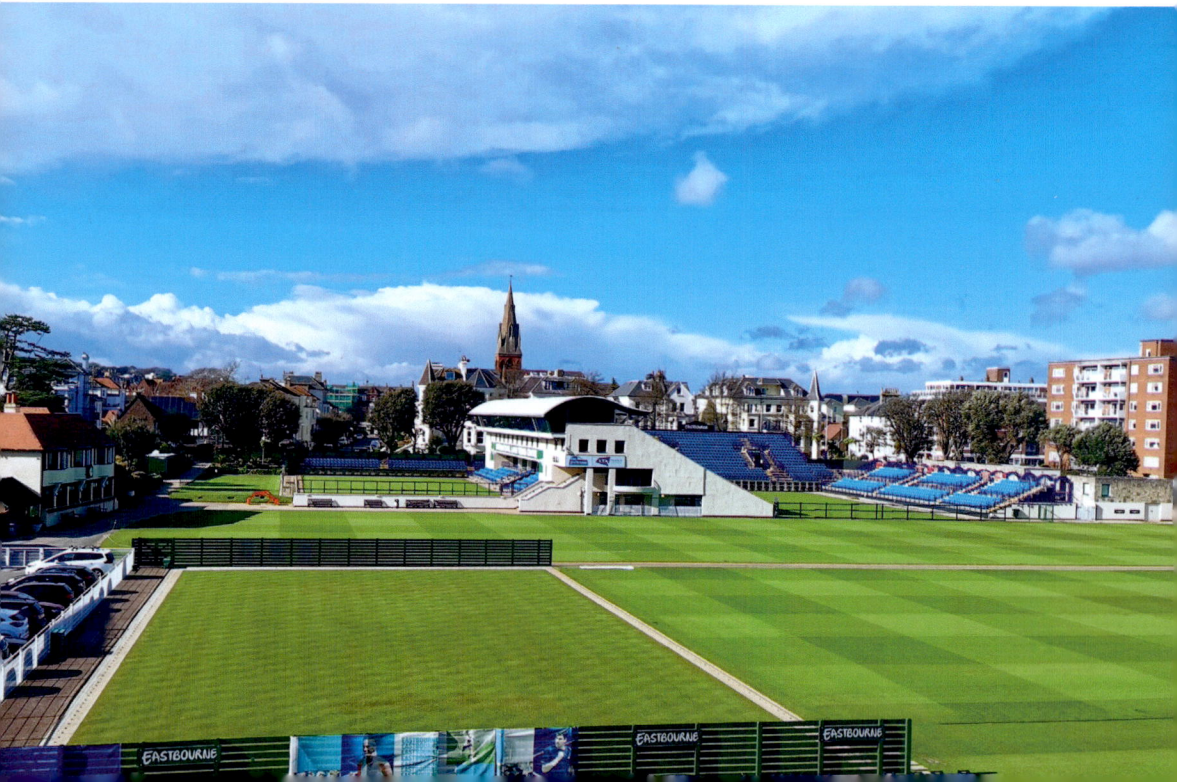

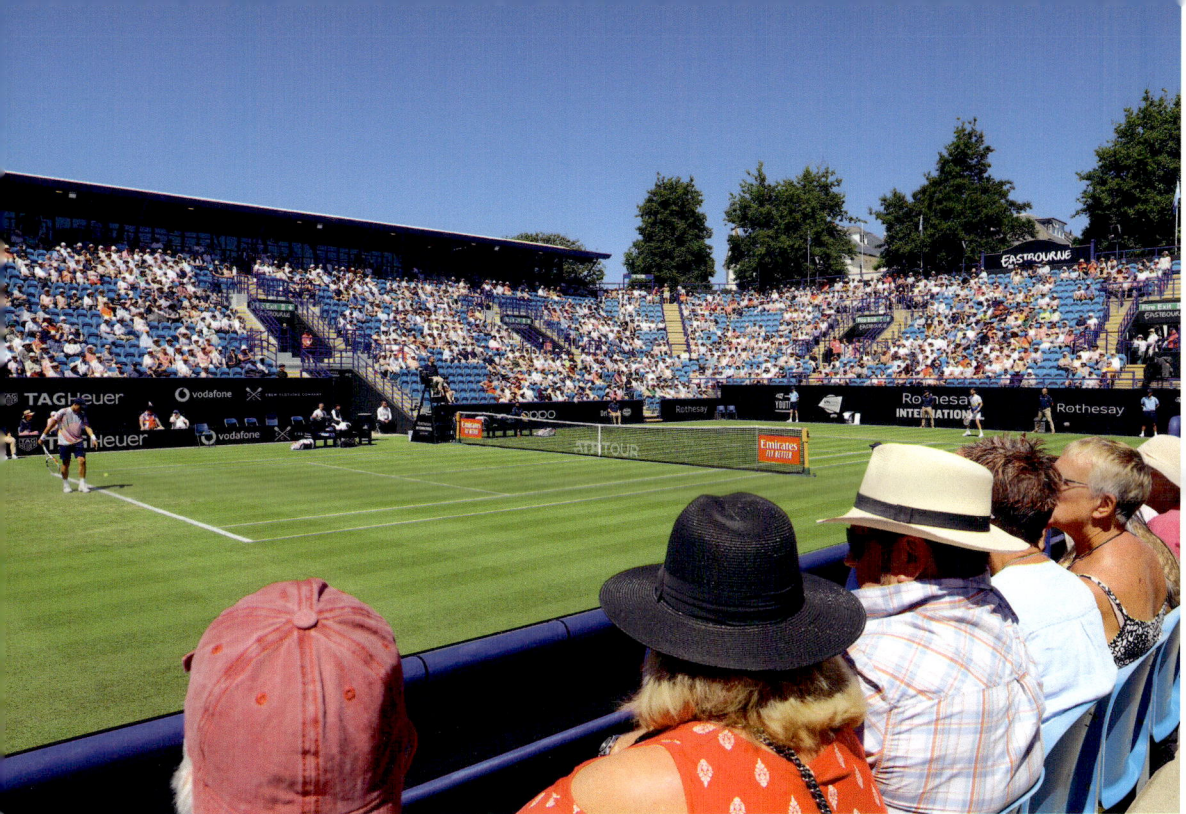

A modern tournament at Devonshire Park. (Eastbourne Borough Council)

The first international of the modern era to be held at Devonshire Park was in 1974 when Chris Evert beat Virginia Wade. The following year Wade beat Billie Jean King in the finals at Eastbourne and in 1978 a young Czech-American player won her first Eastbourne title – Martina Navratilova. She went on to win no less than eleven singles titles at Devonshire Park and in September 2005 she was awarded honorary freedom of Eastbourne. On receiving the award Martina told the press that she was 'humbled and moved by such genuine kindness. I appreciate Eastbourne and Eastbourne appreciates me and I truly feel I am a part of this noble community'.

In 2024 Devonshire Park celebrates its 150th anniversary as a beacon of art and sport.

5

Let There Be Light!

'There is a great outcry in Eastbourne for "more light"'
Eastbourne Gazette, October 1881

Eastbourne Gas Company was established in 1852 and within a year it was supplying gas lighting to 100 private consumers. Shortly afterwards the council established a 'Lighting Committee' to oversee the installation of gas lamps to light the streets after dusk.

The electric light was developed in the 1870s more or less at the same time by Joseph Swan in England and Thomas Edison in the USA. In 1878 Swan installed hydro-electric powered lights into Cragside House in Northumberland and later that year some of the streets in Paris were temporarily lit by electric arc lamps.

On 3 February 1879 a road in Chesterfield was lit by Joseph Swan's new incandescent lightbulb – but it was only lit for one night. A street in Newcastle was the first in the world to be permanently lit by electric lights.

Electric lights were installed in the Floral Hall of Devonshire Park, Eastbourne, in 1881. In October 1881 the *Eastbourne Gazette* reported that 'The brilliancy of the light strikes everyone as marvellous, indeed the vicinity of the park is marked out owing to the unusual brightness of this particular spot during the evening.'

Some residents, however, complained that the light around the park was too bright. Within a few weeks on 11 February 1882 the Eastbourne Electric Lighting Company was established. They immediately sought council approval to carry electric wires 'over streets and houses and in the gas-tubing under the streets for the purposes of carrying electric light into shops and houses'. Naturally the local gas company objected.

The new Electric Company was located at the Old Waterworks at Bedfordwell and they took over the Water Company's boilers to provide power. Street lamps were installed along the seafront but, as such things were new, the company's own staff had to make much of the equipment. Trials were carried out on 1 September 1882 and three days later a mile of the Parade was lit by twenty-two arc lamps. What made this unique was that, unlike other street lamps, for instance those at Brighton, these were lit from a central 'power station' rather than lit by nearby

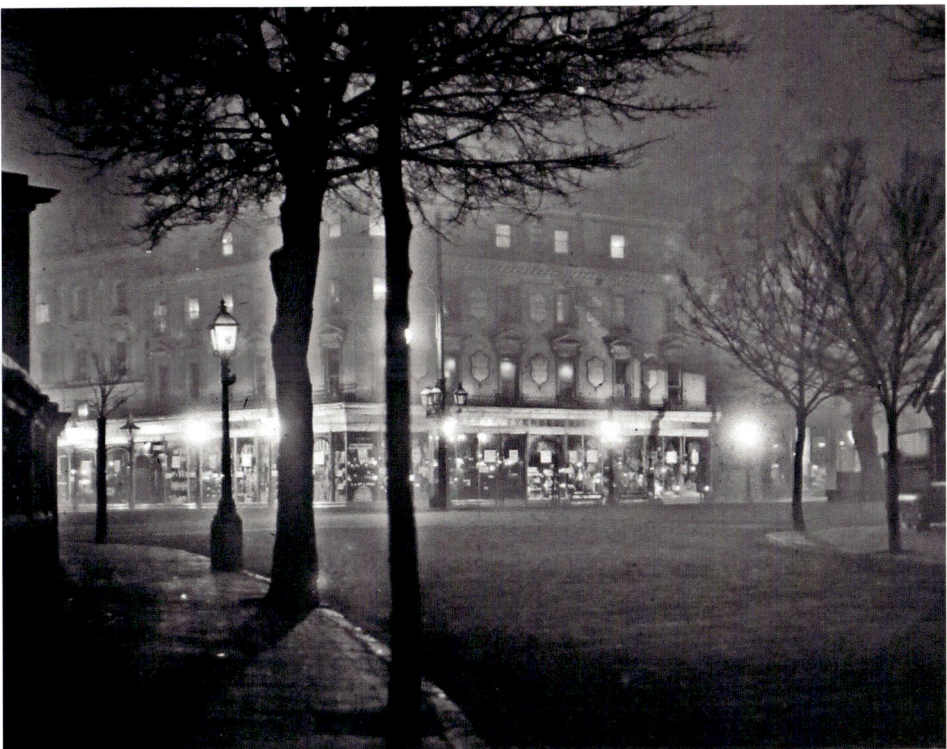

The Memorial Roundabout lit by electricity.

generators. The Edison Station in New York lit street lamps from a power station on exactly the same day as Eastbourne (4 September 1882) but due to the time difference Eastbourne was first! Originally the arc lamps had a very limited life and had to be replaced every day.

In 1884 the Electric Light Company purchased a former brewery in Junction Road and a generating station was built. It was opened in the presence of Marquess T'Seng, the Chinese Ambassador, and was so advanced that representatives of other towns (including Dublin) came to Eastbourne to inspect it. One of the first buildings to benefit from the new power station was the Town Hall. A shop in Grove Road was the first in Eastbourne to be lit by incandescent electric lightbulbs and the Gildredge Hotel in Terminus Road was the first hotel, although these were powered by batteries charged at night.

As you walk around the streets of Eastbourne you may notice evidence of the Eastbourne Electric Light Company as several of their pavement inspection covers can still be seen.

It took a while for the new company to make a profit and in 1890 the first dividends were paid to its shareholders. This did not go unnoticed by the council and they purchased the company on 1 January 1900 for £88,135 (about £9 million today). Councillors were clearly pleased with this acquisition and some

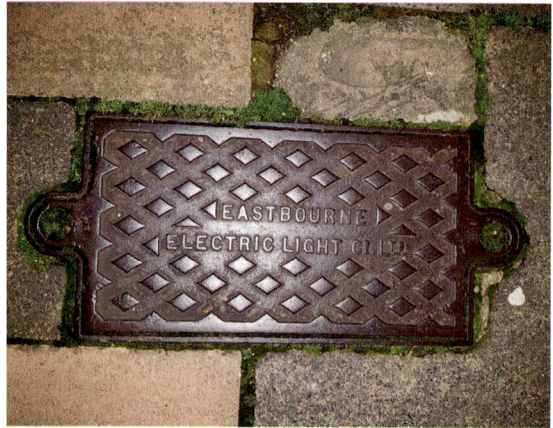 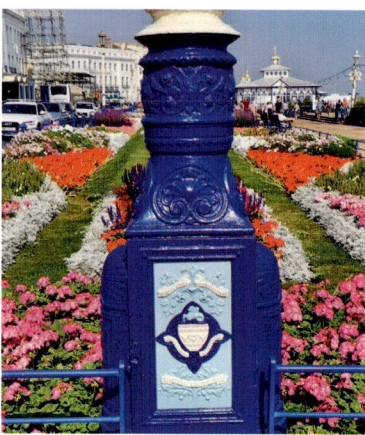

Above left: An Eastbourne Electric Light Company inspection cover at Mill Road at the junction of De Roos Road.

Above right: A lamp post at the Carpet Gardens.

enthusiastically suggested that an electric tram service could be built in the town. This tram scheme was rejected but in 1901 the council invested in new arc lamp posts along the seafront between the pier and the Wish Tower. Several of these still exist and are decorated with the borough coat of arms. Although the beautiful carpet gardens were now illuminated at night there were complaints from visitors that the views from the seafront hotels were obstructed by the bright lighting.

The Corporation appointed a Borough Electrical Engineer, John Kempe Brydges (1868–1954), and under his direction, a modern new power station was built in what was then open countryside at Roselands. As a result the Junction Road power station was closed on 24 July 1902. The new power station was fed by coal, which arrived via a branch line. The electricity supply was extended to Willingdon in 1903.

It is interesting that some of Eastbourne's more wealthy residents petitioned the corporation for a street lamp near their property on the basis that they would pay for the lamp if the council paid for the electricity.

Evidence of the distribution of early street lighting can be seen in green-painted 'Electricity Distribution Cabinets', which can still be seen set into walls around the town. These date from around 1910. Street lighting was a clear success.

Initially electric power was supplied only to commercial customers and to the council for street lighting but in 1922 the scheme was extended to households. Underground substations were built around the town. These were cooled by a fan, which vented from a short green-painted pipe with a cowl on top. Many of these can still be seen around the town.

In 1929 an 'Electricity Showroom' was opened in Grove Road and two years later the supply was extended to Polegate, Hailsham and East Dean. As a result a larger power station was needed and this was built in St Philips Avenue in 1931 and was connected to the new National Grid.

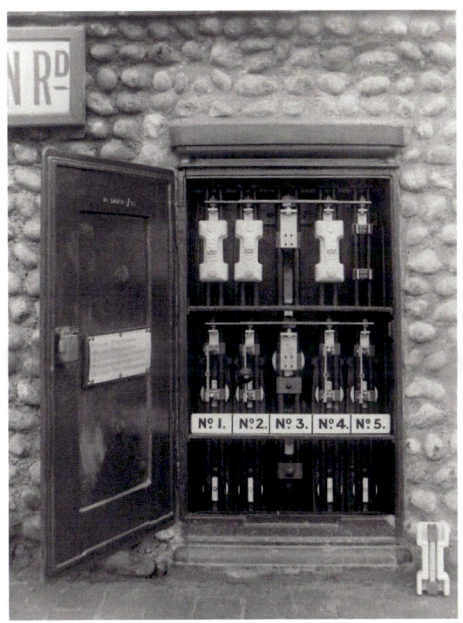
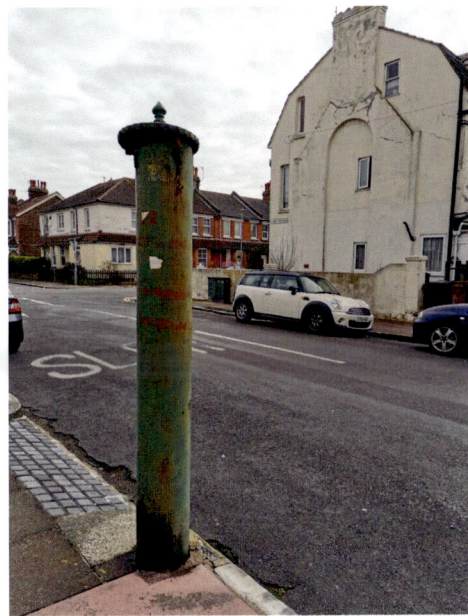

Above left: Street lighting electricity cabinet. (Arlington Road)

Above right: A substation vent in Addingham Road and what is underneath …

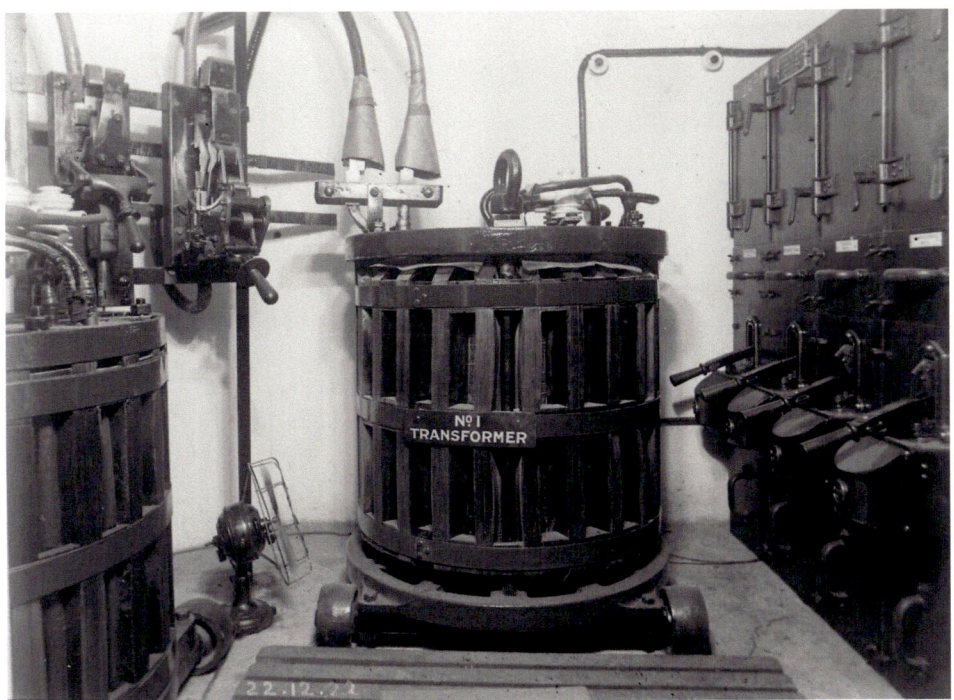

An underground electricity substation.

During the 1930s many of the old street lamps were altered. Motorists complained that the old lantern street lamps spread the light everywhere and made driving difficult at night. As a result the lamps were removed and replaced by 'swan-neck' tops, which were taller but directed the light down onto the road below.

The large works in St Philips Avenue were a clear target for the Luftwaffe during the Second World War and on 26 August 1942 they were virtually destroyed when hit by a 500 lb bomb. The building was rebuilt and on 1 April 1948 the council lost control of the electricity supply when the network was nationalised.

John Brydges retired from his position as the town's Electrical Engineer in April 1939 but he is still remembered as in 1997 Brydge's Close off Roselands Avenue was named after him.

In 2023 one of Eastbourne's oldest street lamps was identified by local enthusiast Bob Cookson. It was discovered in the twitten that leads to the Artizan's Dwellings off South Street. This lantern would have been on one of the original gas lamps in South Street. It would have converted to electricity and then removed in the 1930s when the lamp was moved to light up the nearby twitten. The lamp was looking in a very sorry state until Bob removed, restored and replaced the lamp.

By the way, did you know that you can tell if you are in a conservation area by looking at the street lamps? They are painted black in conservation areas but 'impala beige' elsewhere.

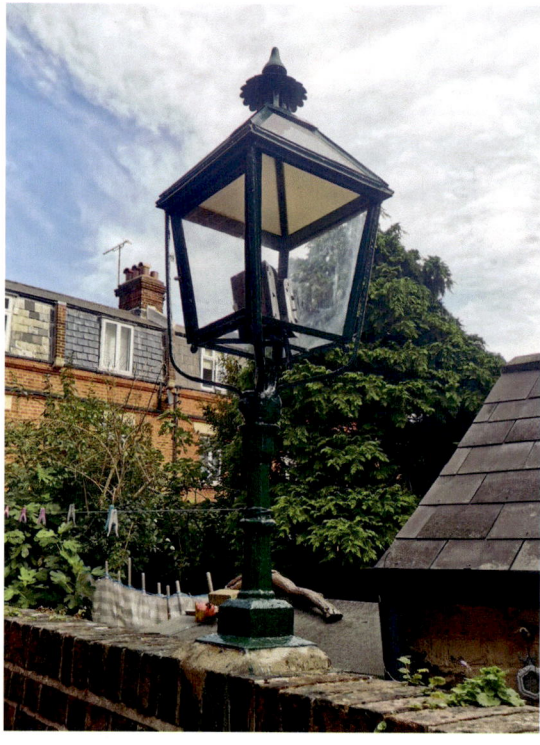

Eastbourne's oldest street lamp restored.

Licence Plates

Whilst researching my family tree I discovered that my ancestors had some interesting occupations. The 1881 census shows that my great-great-grandfather John Roberts was a 'Bath Chairman' and his two sons, John and my grandfather Ebenezer, were 'Drivers of Goat-Chaises'.

A bath chair was a cross between a wheelchair and a taxi. It had been invented by James Heath in 1750 in the city which gave the chair its name. They were often made of wickerwork with two large wheels and a smaller pivoting wheel attached to a long handle. The bath chairman would either pull it along or push it, allowing the passenger to steer. Although originally designed for the infirm, they became popular in seaside resorts and in Eastbourne were often seen on the newly created promenades that stretched from the Redoubt Fortress to the east

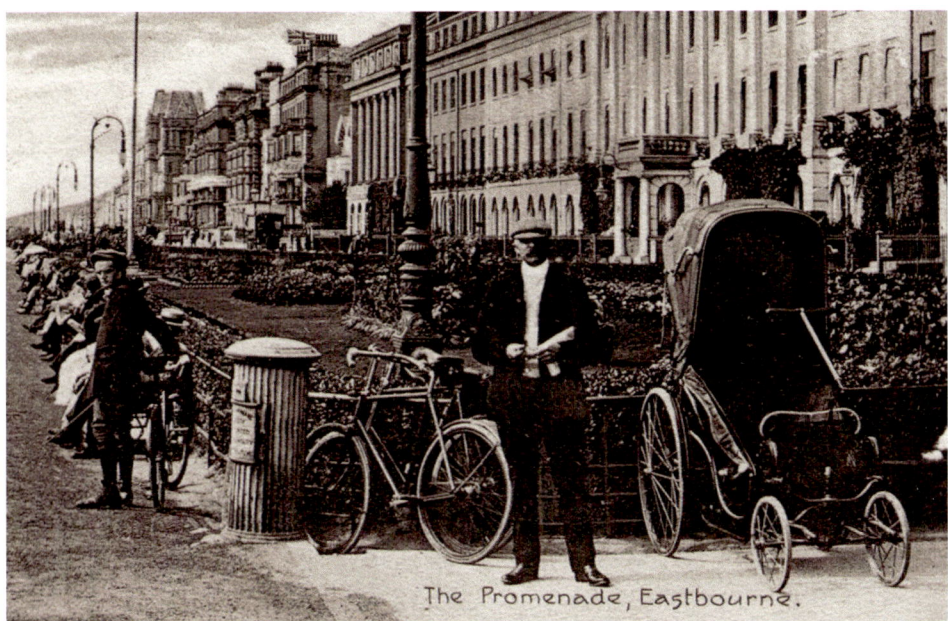

A bath chair near the pier.

and Holywell under the shadow of Beachy Head. In the summer months the work of a bath chairman was hot and demanding but the work was never secure and on many days the bath chairman would not earn enough money to pay for the hire of the chair (in 1919 the cost of a new bath chair was £60, way beyond the means of most local men). The *London News* of 1909 reported that eight Eastbourne bath chairmen had been admitted to the local asylum, 'driven mad through the hardships of their life'.

My ancestor John Roberts was clearly not well-off and his young teenage sons had to work to keep the family fed. They both earned a meagre living by driving a goat-chaise. They provided novelty rides along the prom in a small carriage pulled by two goats.

Again this work was seasonal and in inclement weather there would be little income. This was exacerbated by the fact that there were strict regulations in place as to how and where they could operate. Just like the taxi drivers of today, they had to be licensed and could only ply for hire at specific locations. In 1877, one man was sent to prison for fourteen days for plying a bath chair for hire in Eastbourne without a license. The following year James Newman, the inspector of Hackney Carriages for Eastbourne, reported that he had granted licences for sixty-seven flys (horse-drawn cabs) thirty-six bath chairs, ten saddled ponies, ten goat chaises and five saddled donkeys.

In Eastbourne, Hackney Carriages were divided into three classes: first-class carriages were drawn by one or two horses, could accommodate five passengers and were obliged to take fares up to 5 miles from Eastbourne; second-class carriages were drawn by up to two ponies or asses, could accommodate three passengers and had to carry passengers up to 3 miles; third-class carriages were

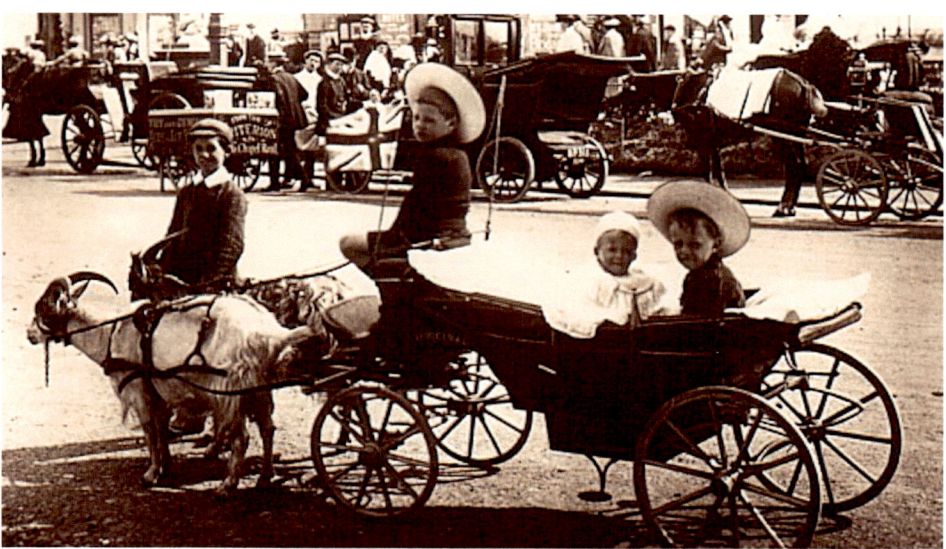

A goat chaise.

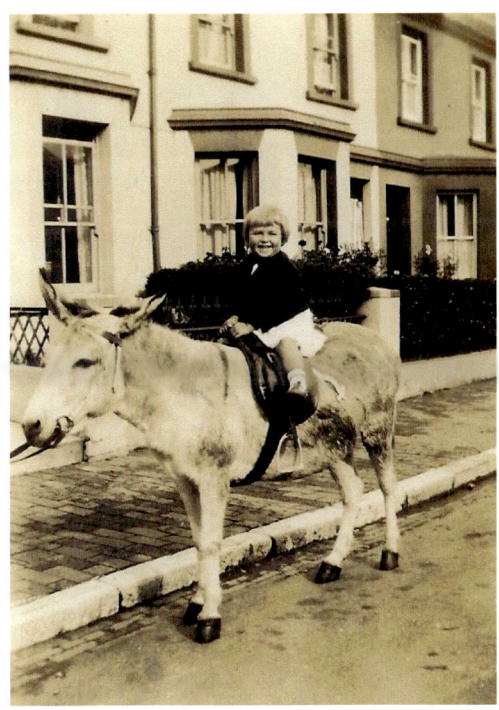

My aunt Sheila on one of my grandfather's saddled donkeys.

pulled by an ass or two goats or by hand, they could take one passenger or two children and were obliged to carry passengers up to 2 miles. The rates depended on time and distance; in 1881 my great-grandfather could charge 8 pence for a mile or a shilling for an hour for use of his goat chaise.

As a result of the Public Health Act 1875 Eastbourne Council installed metal licence plates to the base of walls where licence holders were permitted to stand whilst awaiting hire. Many of these can still be seen around the town centre and seafront and provide a fascinating glimpse into Eastbourne's Victorian past.

We also have an insight into the work of the Eastbourne bath chairmen because one of its ranks, George Meek, wrote a book. I am sure my great-grandfather Ebenezer knew him as both men wrote poetry and prose. I like to think of the two of them discussing politics as they waited for fares at a bath chair stand.

In 1909 Meek was interviewed by local author Arthur Beckett, who was also the editor of the *Eastbourne Gazette*. Beckett described him as 'a man frail of frame, one who looks as if life has not been too kind to him. He is roughly clad, his hands are those of a hard-worker. He is awkward in manner, slow of speech and not always grammatical'. Not the attributes of most authors! Meek, however, would often be seen reading books as he waited for fares beside his bath chair. He particularly enjoyed the work of H. G. Wells and in 1907 wrote to the famous author praising him for *The Time Machine* and *War of the Worlds*. He told Wells that he was a 'Socialist of some fourteen years standing' and that he was involved in holding political meetings not only in Eastbourne – at the Railway Arms in

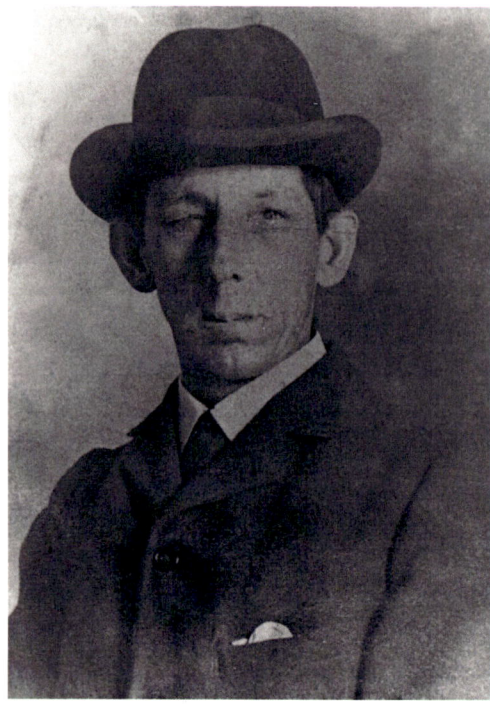

George Meek.

South Street (now the Dolphin) – but also across Sussex and Kent. Wells was obviously impressed and the two became friends. The great author encouraged Meek to write the story of his life and this was published in 1910 as *The Life of a Bath Chairman*, although Meek preferred the title *The Ups and Downs of Life*. When the book was successfully reviewed Meek was amazed, saying 'It is just the simple record of a poor man's life – that is all.' Wells said of the book (of which he wrote the foreword) 'it is precisely because it is a simple record of a poor man's life that will make the author one of the most talked about men of the season – Meek has the stark simplicity of literary greatness about him.'

Meek used the royalties for the book to leave Eastbourne and emigrated to Vancouver but he found the climate in Canada too much for him and, after a year, returned to Eastbourne and his former job.

Today you can follow in the footsteps of George Meek and my great-grandfather Ebenezer Roberts – literally! I mentioned that there were several metal licence plate markers still to be seen in the town. They include plaques marked BCS (Bath Chair Stand) LPS (Luggage Porter Stand) SDS (Saddled Donkey Stand) HCS (Hackney Carriage Stand and GCS (Goat-Chaise Stand). A later one is marked MCS (Motor Char-a-banc stand).

One of the Bath Chair Stand markers was situated in Bolton Road but in March 2023 I noticed that it had gone missing. Having established that it had not been removed by the council, I reported it to the Sussex Police as a 'heritage crime'. After a short investigation the missing plate was recovered and returned to me.

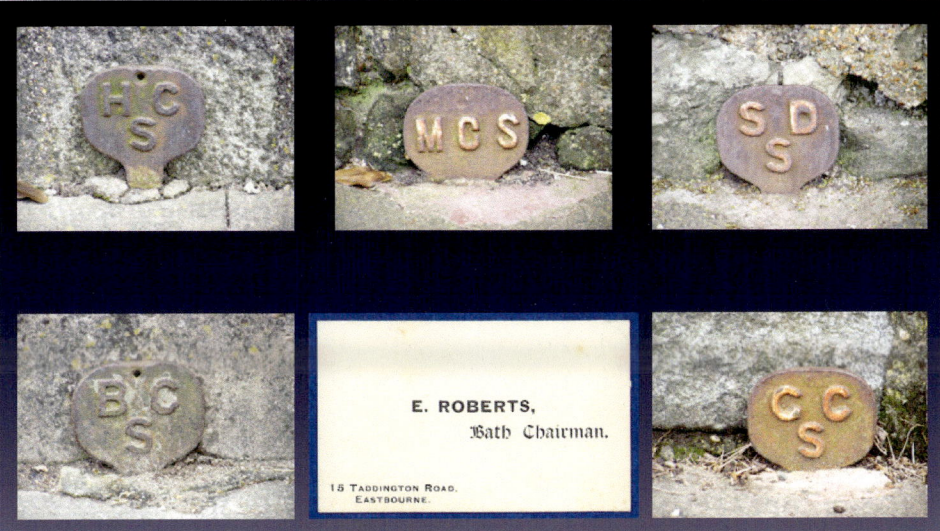

Above: Licence plates.

Right: Restored licence plate in Bolton Road.

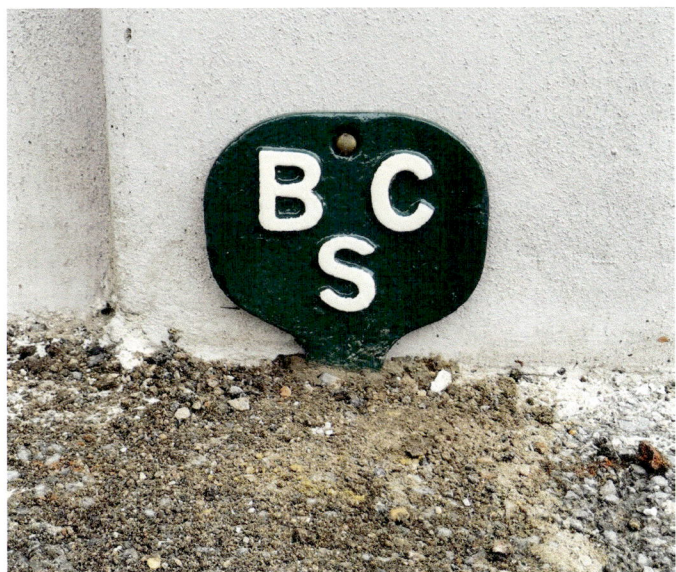

Research established that the original plate was painted green with white lettering and thanks to Bob Cookson it was repainted and restored to its original site.

Following this incident I realised that, unlike other local towns, Eastbourne did not have a 'Local Heritage List' – a list of historic features that are not listed buildings. Following liaison with Heritage Eastbourne at the local council, the list was started in summer 2023. A dedicated team of volunteers scoured the town looking for items of street furniture, letterboxes, street signs and decorated drain covers and hundreds of features have been added to the list. One curious feature of Eastbourne are the sewer vent pipe more often known as stink pipes. These elegant features, up to 9 metres tall, are often overlooked but provided a safety valve, venting methane and other noxious gases from the Victorian sewers.

The Eastbourne Heritage List now boasts an eclectic catalog, including several buildings.

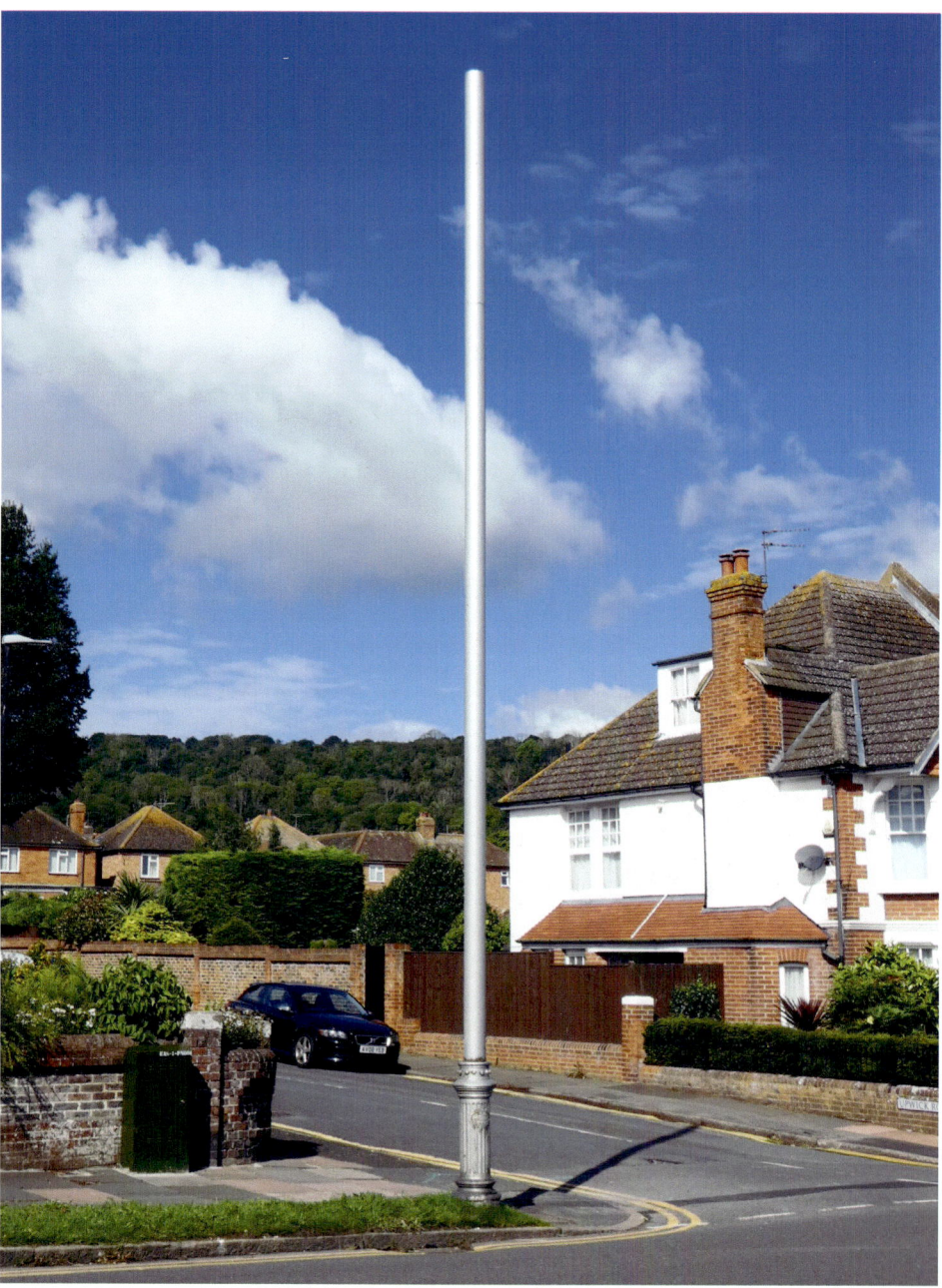

An Eastbourne stink pipe.

Cables to the Continent

A small overlooked building in Meads (now added to the Eastbourne Heritage List) hides a remarkable purpose. It was once a part of an international telegraph communications system that played an important role during the war.

The telegraph was invented by William Cooke and Charles Wheatstone in the 1830s. Electrical pulses along a cable would point needles towards letters on a board so a message could be relayed. The system was first used commercially in 1837 on the railway line between Camden Town and Euston.

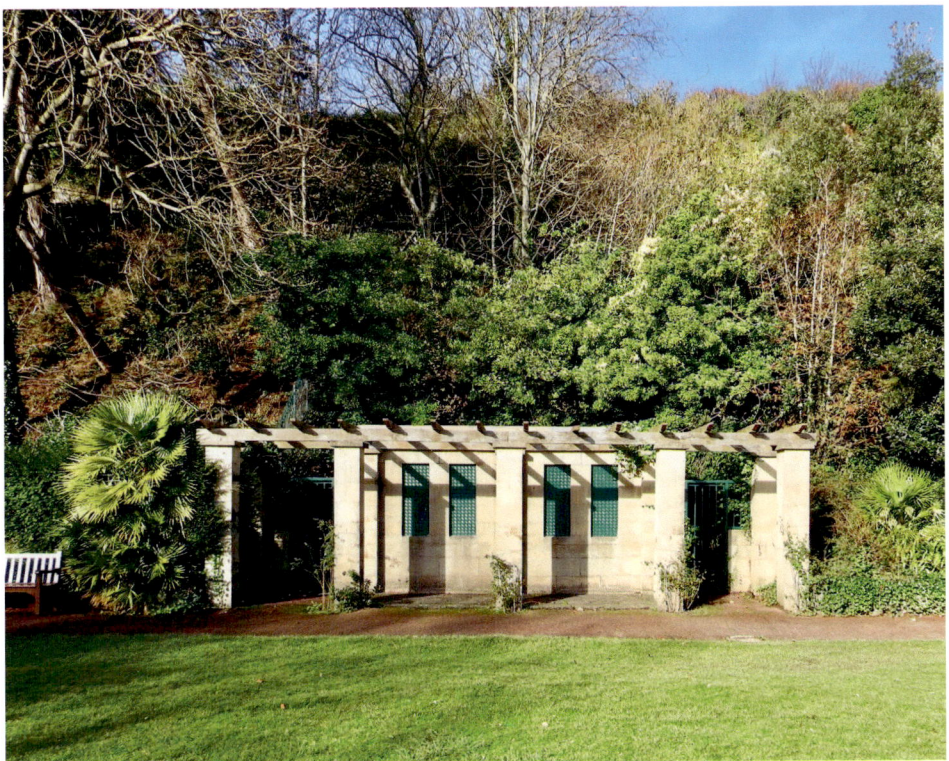

The cable hut at Holywell.

In August 1850 the first cross-channel telegraph cable was laid between Dover and Calais. The cable was insulated with a substance called 'gutta percha' (a rubbery gum of a tree native to Malaysia) and held down with lead weights. Unfortunately the cable broke against the rocks of the French coast and was operational for only a few hours.

In 1851 a second cross-channel cable was successful and this led to other undersea cables being laid around the coast, although some failed within weeks – or sometimes days – of being laid. The valuable cables were not scrapped but lifted and reused. Successful cable routes were later purchased and taken over by the GPO.

Soon the cable companies were looking to connect Europe to America. The amazing project of laying over 2,000 miles of cable across the Atlantic to Newfoundland started in 1854 and was completed on 8 August 1858, after failed attempts to lay the cable in 1857. The cable ran from the west coast of Ireland (then of course part of Great Britain) to Trinity Bay in Newfoundland. The British ship *Agamemnon* and the American ship *Niagara* set off from Ireland each carrying half the entire cable, which was to meet and be joined in the middle. Unfortunately there was a lack of communication between the two companies in England that had manufactured the cable and as a result the 'lay' of the armoured wiring was different on the two sections. One had been made with a 'right hand twist' and the other with a 'left hand twist'. Thus, when the two sections were spliced together, the armouring wires would tend to unravel. When the two ships met mid-Atlantic a 'botch' had to be made to join the two cables.

The first official message to pass electrically across the Atlantic was a congratulations telegram sent to the 15th President of the United States, James Buchanan, by Queen Victoria on 18 August 1858. The message actually took seventeen hours and forty minutes to reach its destination, which at that time was the fastest message to be sent on earth! The cable, the culmination of four years of work, lasted just a few weeks but a new cable of a much-improved design laid in 1866 by the SS *Great Eastern* was far more successful.

In 1861 an undersea telegraph cable was laid between Dieppe and Eastbourne by the Submarine Telegraph Company. It was originally due to land at Newhaven but maybe the port was too busy – the surrounding waters had to be regularly dredged which may have damaged the cable. The actual cable had originally been laid between Sardinia and Africa but when this link failed the cable was lifted and reused for the Eastbourne link. The cable was operational for many years, although in 1874 over 20 miles of it had to be replaced.

Although known as the 'Beachy Head to Dieppe Cable', the English end terminated at a small cable building at Holywell, close to the old Gore Chalk Pit.

When the area was later prettified and the chalk pit became The Sunken Italian Gardens, the old hut was deemed to be an eyesore and the GPO were persuaded to disguise it by having fake windows painted on and a rose-covered pergola placed against it.

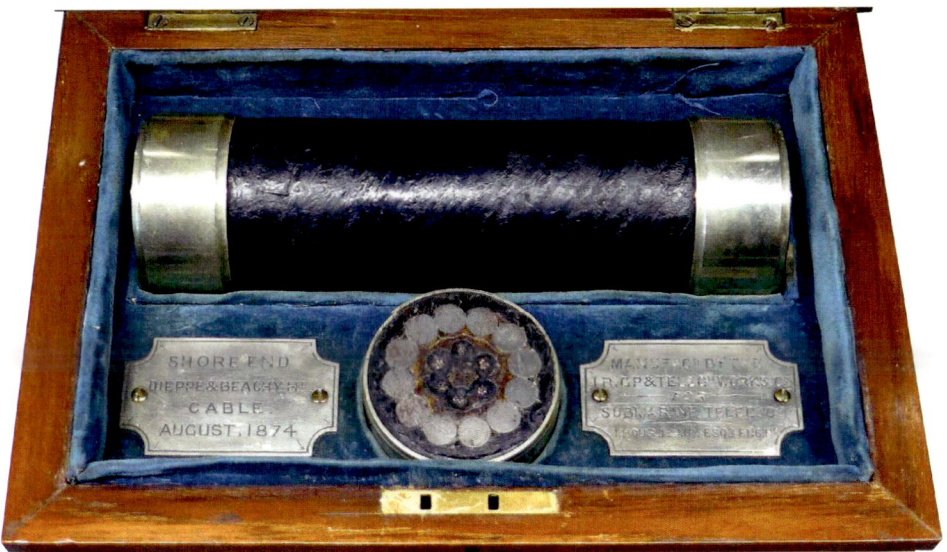

A part of the 'Beachy Head' cable.

Nine years after the Eastbourne cable, another was laid in 1870 between Cap d'Antifer (between Le Havre and Fecamp in Normandy) and Birling Gap. This cable was in use until the 1920s, by which time it had been taken over by the GPO but it didn't last long and by 1930 the cable hut had fallen into the sea due to cliff erosion.

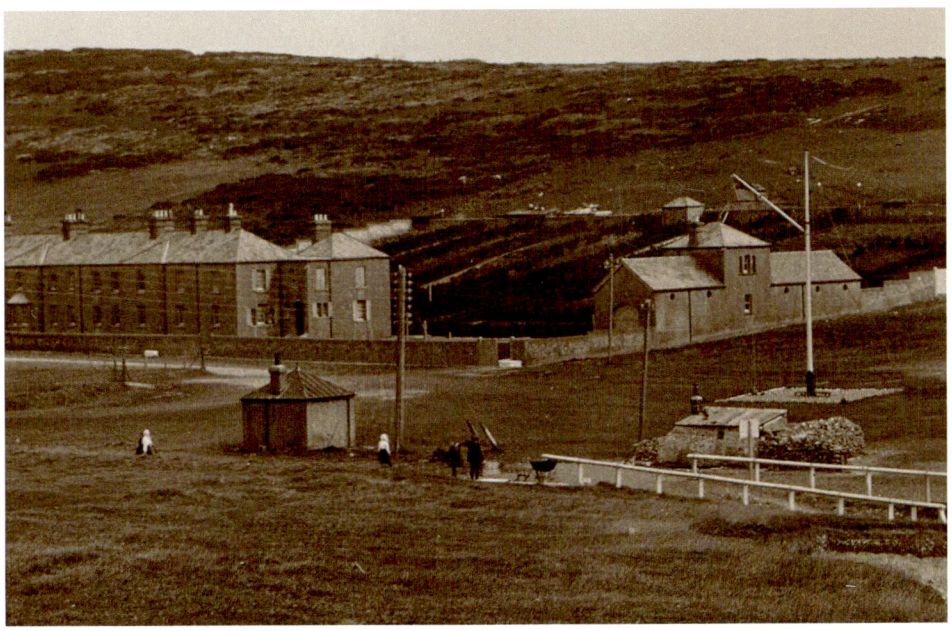

The cable hut at Birling Gap (foreground).

In 1900 the Anglo-America Cable Company working in conjunction with the French equivalent of the GPO (PTT – Postes, Telegraphes et Telephones) constructed a third local cross-channel cable, which was laid between Le Havre and Cuckmere Haven. The main use of this cable was to link France to the USA via Anglo America's transatlantic cable.

The Cuckmere Haven cable hut is located between the Coastguard Cottages and the beach but is in a perilous position and may soon suffer the fate of the Birling Gap hut and fall into the sea.

Within weeks of the outbreak of the First World War a telegraph cable between Borkum on the German North Sea coast and Vigo in Spain was cut by the British and commandeered. It was then relaid between Cuckmere Haven and St Nazaire in Brittany for cross-channel military use. At the same time the area around Cuckmere Haven had been militarised and nearby Seaford became a garrison town with two massive military camps. As early as 1915 Cuckmere Haven was being used for firing practice by Irish troops. One can only think how nervous the GPO was, having so many munitions exploding near their precious cable!

Due to the war, the GPO added four further wires between Cuckmere Haven and France in 1917. After the sinking of the SS *Lusitania* in April 1917, the USA joined

The cable hut at Cuckmere Haven.

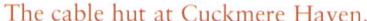

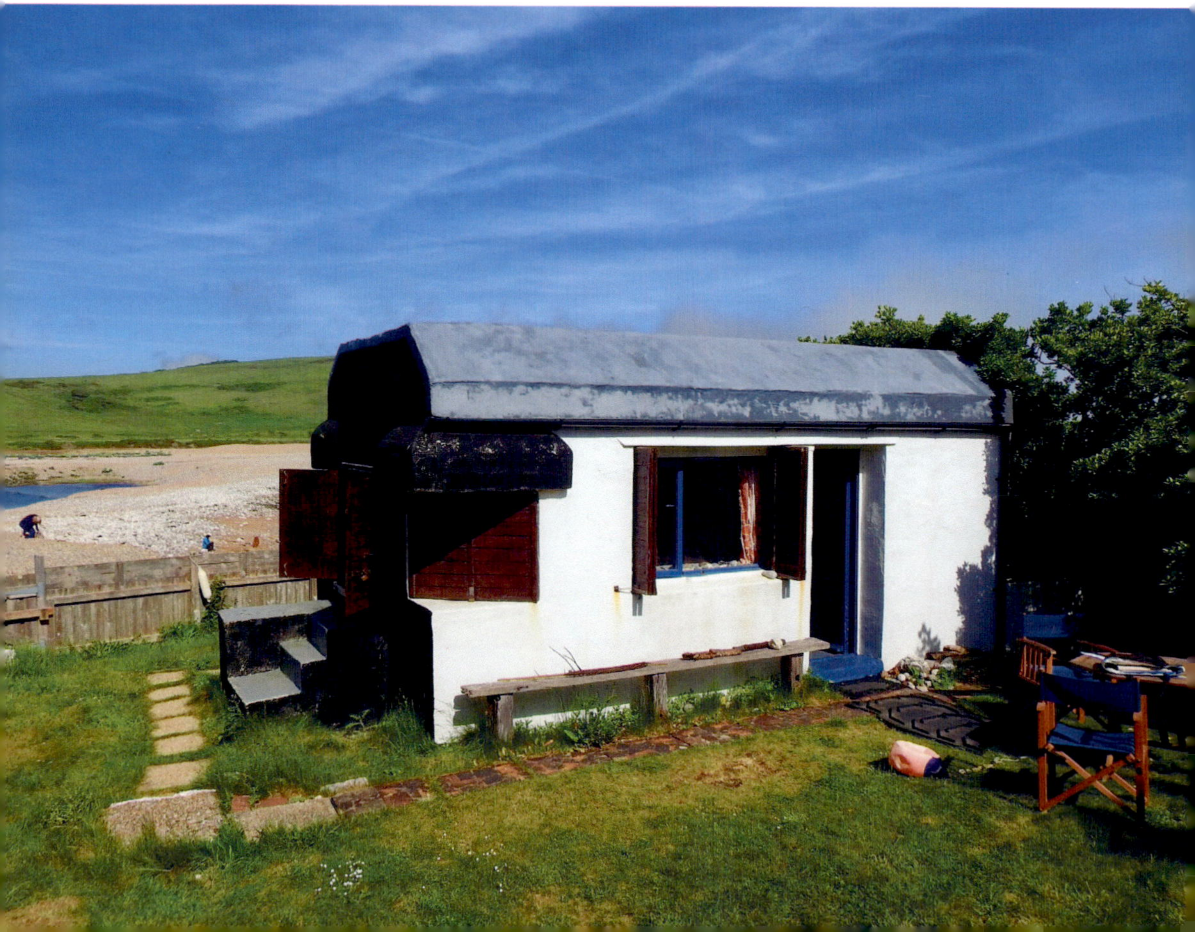

the war and thousands of American troops were sent to France. Communication between the warzones and the USA was vital and in November 1917 Colonel C. S. Wallace, the Chief Signal Officer for the US Army, visited Sussex to see how communications could be improved.

Colonel Wallace made arrangements with the GPO to lay further cables between Cuckmere Haven and France and immediately take over the cables between Eastbourne and Le Havre. The Eastbourne route was first used on 26 November 1917 when a message from General John J. Pershing, the Commander of the American Expeditionary Force in Europe was sent to the US Embassy in London from his French HQ in Chaumont.

During the Second World War in June 1940 the Germans were quickly overrunning France. The British military were concerned that the undersea cables between Sussex and France could be used by German submarines as navigational aids, so within days of the German occupation of Normandy a secret plan called Operation *Quixote* ensured that the cables between England and France were cut and removed. The cables from Eastbourne were cut on the beach and the ones from Cuckmere Haven were cut by the Post Office cable ship *Alert* and never reconnected.

Today the Holywell cable hut can still be seen, although there is no trace of its former use inside. However, it is a reminder of when Eastbourne was part of the cutting edge technology.

The Coming of Cars

The original motor cars were based on horse-drawn carriages. The Petroleum Act of 1862 required local authorities to license the storage and sale of petroleum spirit (benzoline). In 1871 William Morris Caffyn was issued a licence to store benzoline in a shed at the rear of his ironmongers shop in Seaside Road. By 1896 there were five authorised sellers of petroleum spirits in Eastbourne, although it is likely that much of this petrol was being used for lighting. It was this year when many Eastbournians saw their first motor car when a flower-decorated motor car took part in the annual Eastbourne *Battle of the Flowers* parade.

The *Eastbourne Gazette* of 18 November 1896 reported that 'The motor car is going to revolutionize the street locomotion of the world – although it does

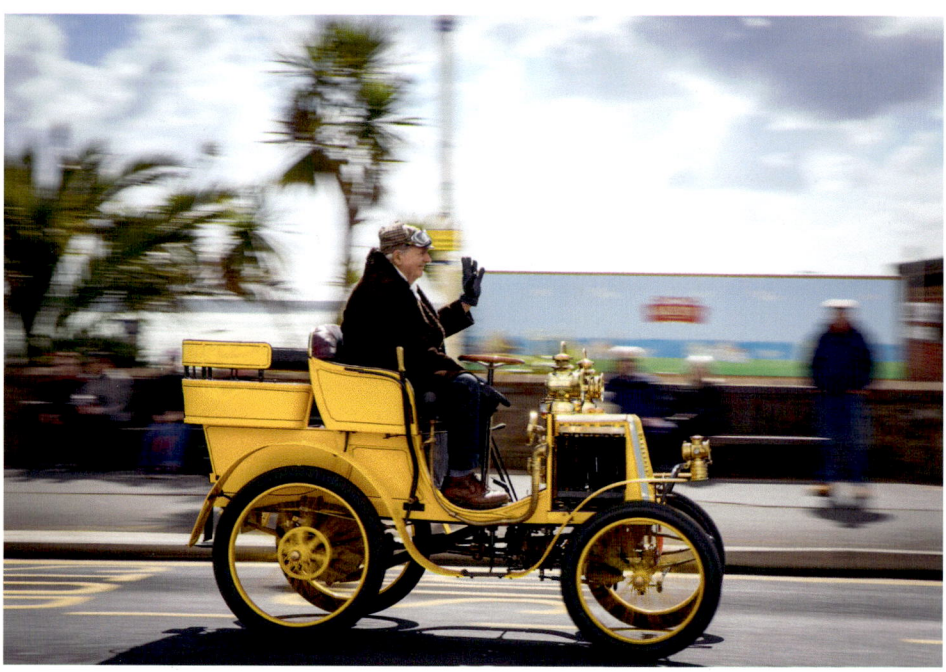

A vintage car on Eastbourne prom. (Eastbourne Borough Council)

not appear to have made much difference in Eastbourne. However a well-known business in the town will shortly deliver goods by means of a motor-car and then we will be able to see if they catch on. One thing to recommend the motor-car is that it will not run away or gnaw on the bark of tress then left unattended in the street!'

Two years later in 1898 the Inspector for Weights and Measures reported to Eastbourne Council that there was a new form of fuel called 'petrol', which was used in 'motor-cars'. By 1900 the town had eight establishments licenced to store and sell petrol. Five years later there were twenty-two licenced garages and by 1914 there were forty. This indicates how quickly the new-fangled motor car became popular. Unlike other councils, however, the licences were granted on the basis that motor cars could only be refuelled on licenced premises and not across the pavement. There were still few motor cars about. In February 1896 the *Eastbourne Gazette* reported 'the strange sight of a spick and span motor-car in Terminus Road'.

The first owner of a motor car in Eastbourne was a Mr George Stockman, who had purchased his car for £375 (about £35,000 today). He ran a confectionary business in Cornfield Road and lived in Upper Avenue. Although a member of the Eastbourne Bicycling Club in 1897, he became fascinated by motor cars. His first

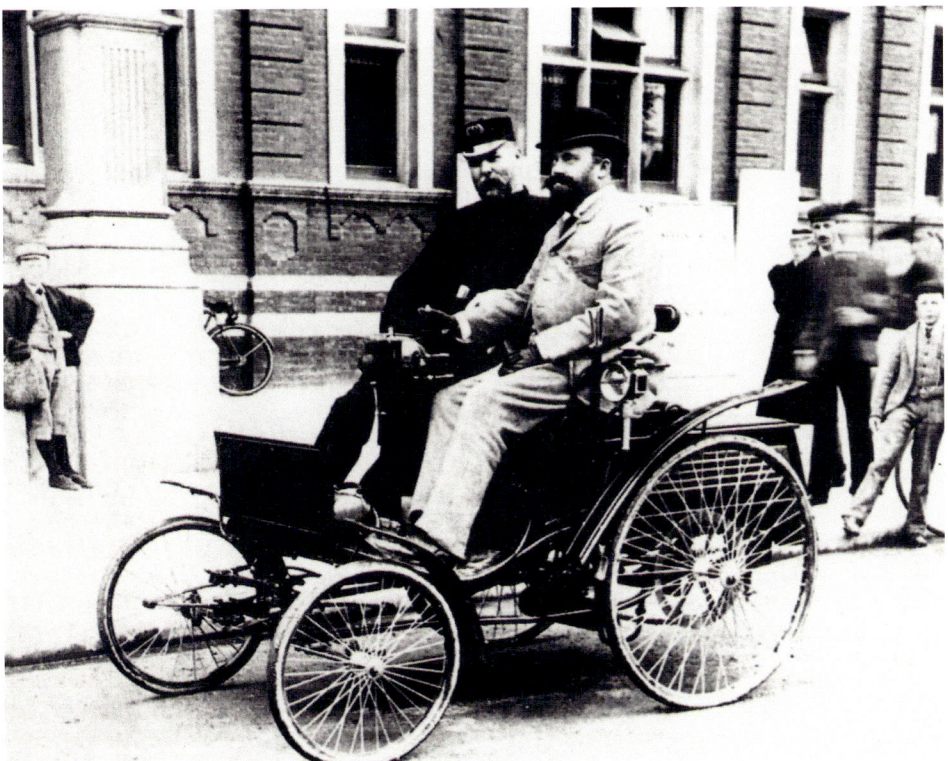

Harry Plumb and George Stockman in the Benz Velocipede.

car was a 3-hp Benz Velocipede and he is seen here in his car in front of the Town Hall in 1898. His passenger is the Eastbourne Chief Constable, Harry Plumb. In September 1899 Plumb called Stockman to Eastbourne Magistrates to act as an 'expert witness' in a case of speeding. It was alleged that a young Texan motorist had been seen driving his car at 20 mph in Cavendish Place. The American complained that Plumb had called a witness (Stockman) who was a personal friend and that no one in the world could drive a motor car at 20 mph! He was found guilty and fined 10 shillings.

The second car owner in Eastbourne was Mr James John Hissey, who in October 1898 applied for planning permission to build a 'motor-shed' at his house in Trevin Towers. This is probably the first 'garage' in Eastbourne, although Hissey called it his a 'motor-car stables'. The council sent an inspector to check the building to ensure that it was suitable. In May 1899 Hissey wrote to a friend telling him about a motor trip to Reigate but 'the first thing I did after arriving home was to stable the motor but I knocked my headlamp which smashed'.

Another early Eastbourne motorist was General Hugh Rose of Silverdale Road, a veteran of the Anglo-Indian Wars. Apparently he was once seen stationary in his motor car unable to persuade it up the slight incline from Devonshire Park to

Hissey (1847–1921) was a travel writer (and ghost hunter) who used his 4-hp Daimler motor car to travel across the country. Several of his books including *An English Holiday with Car and Camera* (1908), *The Charm of the Road* (1910) and *A Leisurely Tour of England* (1913) set off from Eastbourne.

Hissey was the son of a wealthy Yorkshire landowner and in 1880 he married Elizabeth Bouch (whose father Thomas had designed the infamous Tay Railway Bridge which collapsed in 1879, causing the death of over seventy people). On her death in 1885 Hissey moved to Raven's Mead in Carlisle Road, Eastbourne. He was a keen artist (he illustrated his own books) and during classes in Eastbourne met his second wife Katherine Pidcock. They married at St Saviour's Church in 1890 and he designed and built their house, Trevin Towers in Gaudick Road, Eastbourne, where he lived until his death.

Hissey (known to his friends as JJ) had business interests in the USA and, after one visit, bought back a tobacco plant, which he successfully managed to grow in Eastbourne. On 23 September 1886 he wrote to a friend saying 'whilst writing this I am indulging in my first pipe of home-grown tobacco weed'.

Trevin Towers was later to become a rest home (my great-grandmother Bessie died there in 1953). Hissey's garage is now a Grade II listed building.

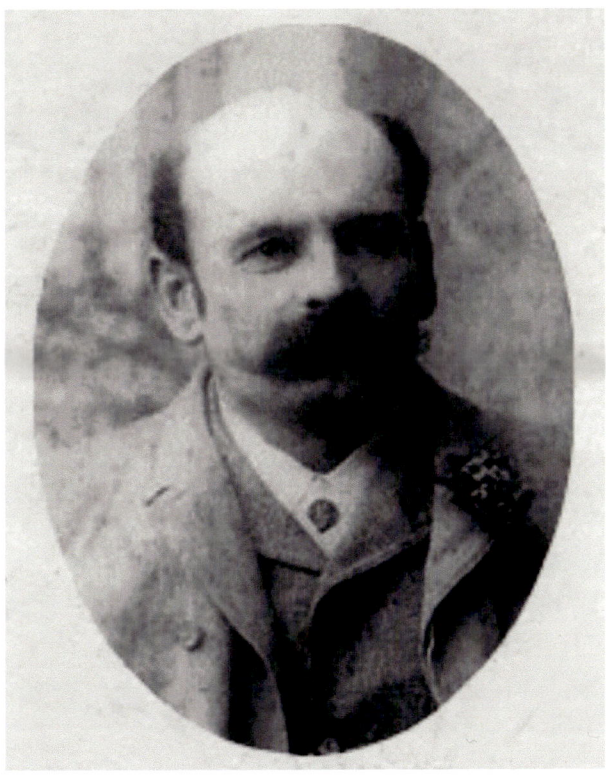

James John Hissey.

Compton Street. Some nearby luggage porters saw his predicament and helped push the machine onto level ground where it chugged off towards the Town Hall.

At 9 p.m. on 24 January 1899, Alwyn Andrews of The Avenue was seen by Eastbourne's Chief Constable Harry Plumb driving a motor car along Terminus Road at a 'furious speed so as to endanger the lives of her Majesty's subjects' (between 10 and 16 mph). Several witnesses said they had to 'scamper' to avoid being hit. Andrews denied the charge but was found guilty and fined £5 (about £400 today) with an alternative of serving fourteen days' imprisonment.

The following month the *Eastbourne Chronicle* reported: 'Conviction upon conviction are fast bringing the motor-car into disrepute. If the motor car has come to stay drivers need to cultivate care and solicitude for others for which, at present they are sublimely indifferent.'

In 1900 an Eastbourne hotel replaced their 'pair-horse bus' with a motor car. Eastbourne's cab men were worried and asked the council not to allow licences for motor cars to be used as taxis. Although early car manufacturers like Benz and Daimler were importing their pioneering new vehicles, several local Eastbourne carriage makers began to make their own versions. Silas Guy & Sons were established in 1863 but due to an increase of business in making motor cars 'to our own design' moved their Victoria Carriage Works from Pevensey Road to larger premises in Susans Road in 1906. Saxon's Garage was an even older

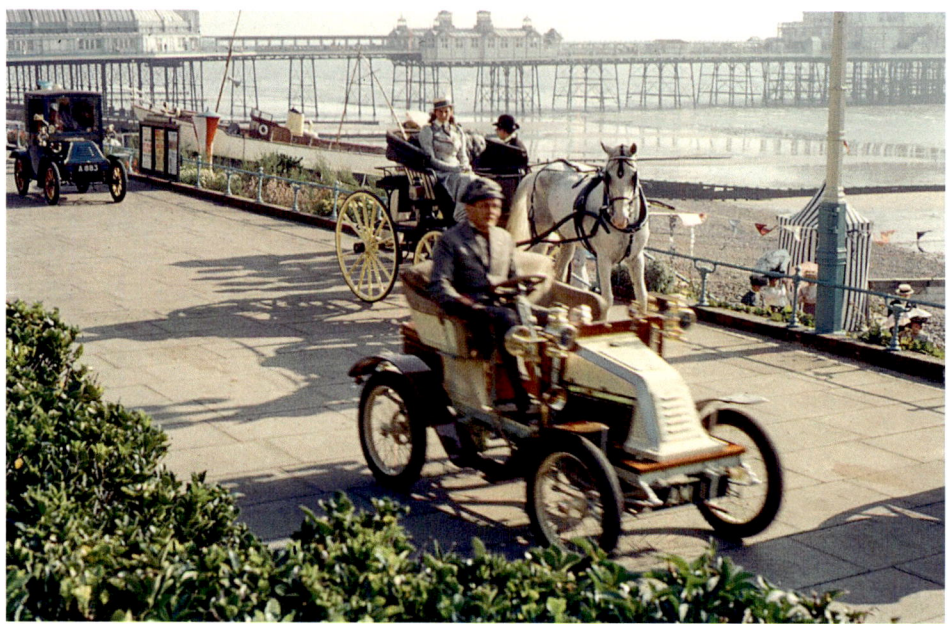

Vintage cars on Eastbourne prom during the filming of *Half a Sixpence* in 1966.

business having been started by George Saxon (senior) in 1856. They had a garage and works in Seaside and designed a wicker 'postal hand-car' for Eastbourne post office. These were so successful that the design was used by the post offices in Africa.

In 1916, when fourteen years old, my grandmother Bessie Gordon gained a position as a secretary at Saxon's Garage. She worked six days a week for a wage

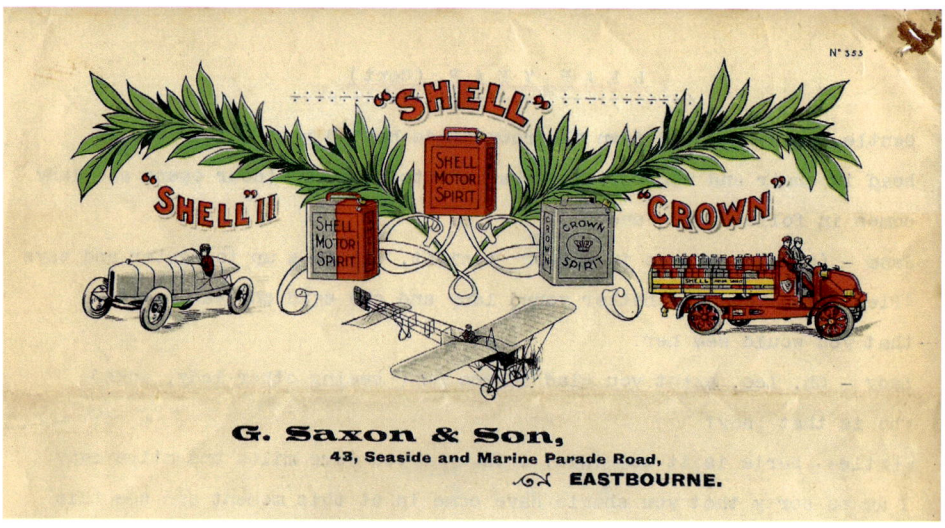

Saxon Garage letterhead.

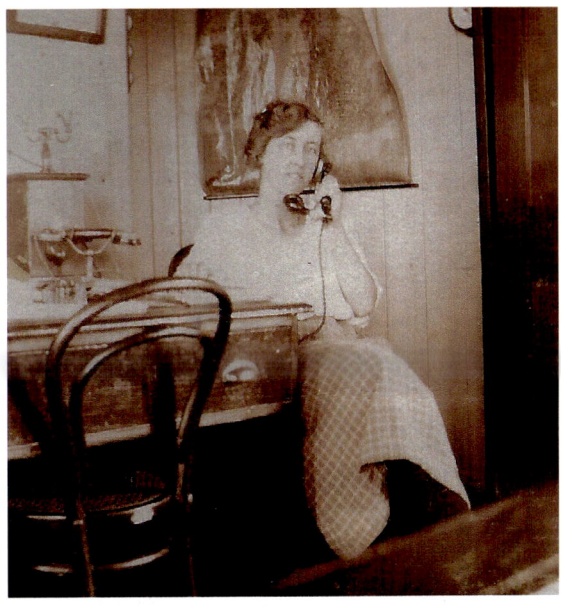

My grandmother Bessie in the office.

of 7 shillings. I am lucky to have her diaries at this time and it is clear that she got on well with her boss. Although she typed letters, did the accounting, paid the staff wages, etc, the work was not onerous and she was often able to do some sewing at work or pop down to the library for a book. Saxon's helped her to attend the Eastbourne Technical Institute where she learned bookkeeping and shorthand (by the age of sixteen she was able to type sixty words per minute).

My grandmother's typing was fast but so were many of the cars on Eastbourne's roads. In 1913, following the deaths of two small girls in Eastbourne, the council was urged to introduce a 10 mph speed limit. A petition was handed into the Town Hall but was rejected. The reasons for refusal given by the council included:

- The roads of Eastbourne were fairly wide.
- The Borough Police had sufficient powers to prosecute dangerous driving.
- A 10 mph speed limit would encourage motorists to drive at this speed.
- There were no speed limits in most other seaside resorts.
- The AA had requested their members to drive with care when visiting Eastbourne.

Alderman Martin told the council that if a speed limit were introduced in Eastbourne, the town would lose many visitors.

Several Eastbourne motorists, however, made their name through speed. Local butcher, Henry Leeson (1898–1932) loved exciting sports. Henry was a successful farmer and butcher with eight shops across the town. In August 1930 he qualified as a pilot at the Cinque Ports Flying Club but his passion was for motoring, having started to drive in 1906.

On 3 March 1931 Henry was driving a green 12-hp racing car between Pevensey and Pevensey Bay when he lost control. His car left the road and hit the wall of Fence Bridge. The local vicar, Reverend Jones, witnessed the incident and estimated the car was travelling at over 60 mph. The driver, however, told a subsequent court hearing that his speed was about 15 mph and that he swerved to avoid a dog which had run out of the bushes in front of his car. This seems unlikely, especially as the car was described as being wrecked after the crash and none of the witnesses saw a dog. However, the magistrates dismissed the case.

Henry started motor racing later that year and in September participated in the Lewes Speed Trials on Race Hill (named after the racecourse). There were several car races: Henry came first in the Super Sporting Cars Unlimited race, second in two other races and third in three other races, either driving a MG Midget or a Bentley.

Henry had married in 1924 and his wife Edith said that his one wish in life was to race at the Brooklands Motor Racing Circuit near Weybridge in Surrey. He was to get his wish in June 1932 when he entered the British Junior Car Club's 1,000 Mile Race. Sixty-three motorists including four women took part in driving 400 laps of the iconic banked motor circuit over two days. Henry was driving an MG Midget at about 70 mph when it suddenly veered across the track and hit a parapet. The car was wrecked and Henry was killed. Edith told the inquest that her husband had been overexcited in taking part in the race. His body was returned to Eastbourne and buried at Ocklynge Cemetery.

An Aston Martin racing car used by Henry Leeson. (Steve Waddingham)

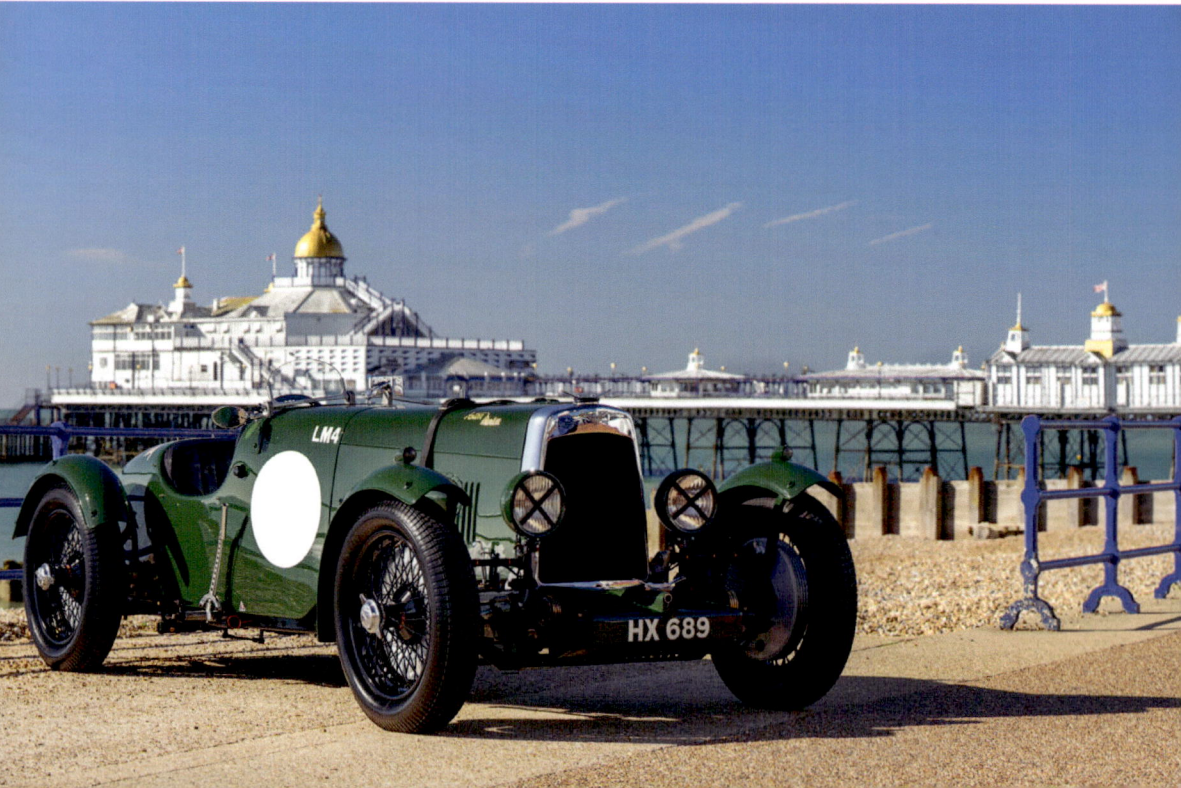

Another sporting motorist was Alfred Thomas Goldie Gardner (1890–1958). During the First World War he served in the Royal Field Artillery and in 1917 was awarded the Military Cross for bravery. Later that year, however, he was seriously injured in an aeroplane accident and was sent to a military hospital in Eastbourne to recover. He needed a stick to walk for the rest of his life. He clearly enjoyed speed and in 1924 purchased his first car in order to take part in races at the iconic Brooklands motor circuit. He later bought an MG car and was to be associated with the make for many years. In 1935 Goldie was Malcolm Campbell's team manager for his world land-speed record attempts on Daytona Beach in the USA. Gardner himself broke many speed records including being the first person to travel at over 200 mph on a German autobahn. During the Second World War both men were tasked with helping to evacuate the royal family to safe houses (or rather safe castles) in case of a Nazi invasion. During the D-Day landings Goldie served on General Eisenhower's staff.

After the war, Gardner set many speed records on the Bonneville Salt Flats in the USA; in 1951 alone he broke sixteen international and American land-speed records there. The following year he crashed during a world record attempt and a head injury caused him to retire to Denton Road, Eastbourne. Goldie died at St Mary's Hospital in 1958 and was buried at Ocklynge cemetery. The *Eastbourne Herald* reported that he was a man of rare courage and a friend of people of all walks of life from princes and prime ministers to the man in the street. Goldie loved Eastbourne and would regularly be a judge at the annual Concours D'Elegance.

In 1904 it was first suggested that Eastbourne host a Concours D'Elegance, which is basically a motor-car beauty contest. It took many years to organise this and the first was held on 10 September 1930, with all monies raised being donated to the Princess Alice Hospital. 143 entries were submitted from motorists across the country – the furthest driving down from Berwick on Tweed. The judges included Captain Malcolm Campbell and Captain Neville Stack, who entertained the crowds with a thrilling acrobatic display in his aeroplane. The guest of honour, Sir Alan Cobham KBE DFC, declared the event to be a huge success and Eastbourne was compared to the French resorts of Deauville and Nice. Sir Alan

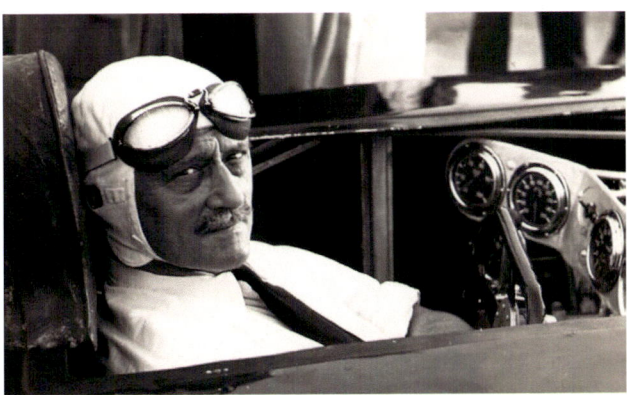

Goldie Gardner.

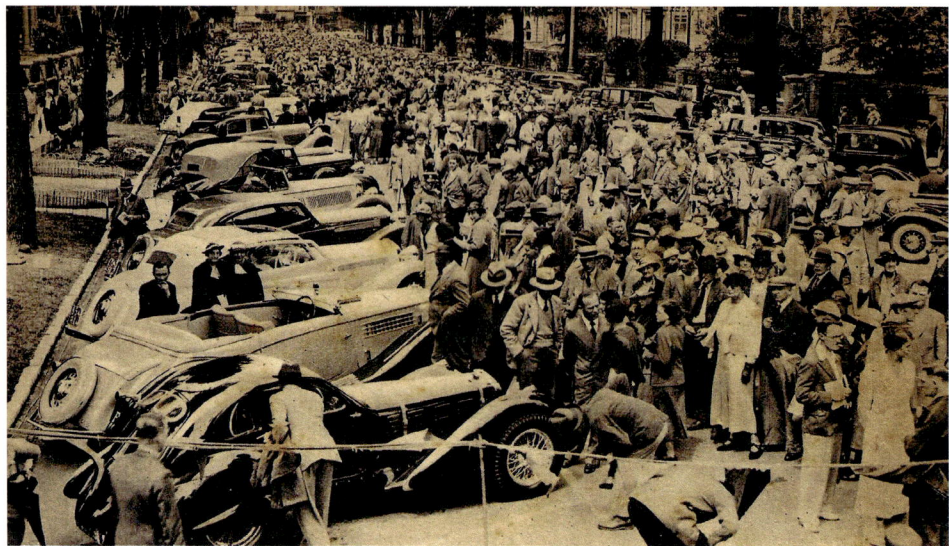

The Concours D'Elegance in Devonshire Place.

proposed that Eastbourne hold the event regularly and should also consider a similar event for aeroplanes.

The Concours D'Elegance was held annually but by 1936 had been moved to Devonshire Place, which was decorated with flags. By this time the event had become famous and several of the entries had travelled from France. The *Eastbourne Chronicle* reported that the French entries were 'accompanied by a bevy of typically chic French ladies whose fashionable dresses were a source of much interest to the lady onlookers'. Winning cars were assembled in front of the Grand Hotel where prizes were distributed by the mayor and 'Hollywood starlets' who had travelled to Eastbourne whilst staying in the Dorchester Hotel in London.

In the 1950s the Concours D'Elegance was moved again and was held inside at the Winter Garden. One of the official photographers at this time was a local doctor, John Bodkin-Adams, who was to later be arrested on suspicion of murder.

One Eastbourne motor engineer did his best to make motoring safer and more glamorous. Pietro Rossi was born in Italy but settled in Eastbourne when he married a local girl in 1919. He had a garage at No. 37 Ceylon Place, from where he hired cars to visitors. Pietro was an inventor and designed several aids for motoring. These included a metal anti-dazzle windscreen blind, which could be pulled across the windscreen to diminish the glare of oncoming headlights at night. It must be remembered that these were the days when motor cars had one set of undimmable headlights and no 'side-lights'. Bright headlamps whilst driving at night was obviously a problem so Pietro also designed a means of dimming car headlights. This took the form of screens which could be lowered over the lights 'operated by the twist of a handle from the driver's seat'. However, the invention

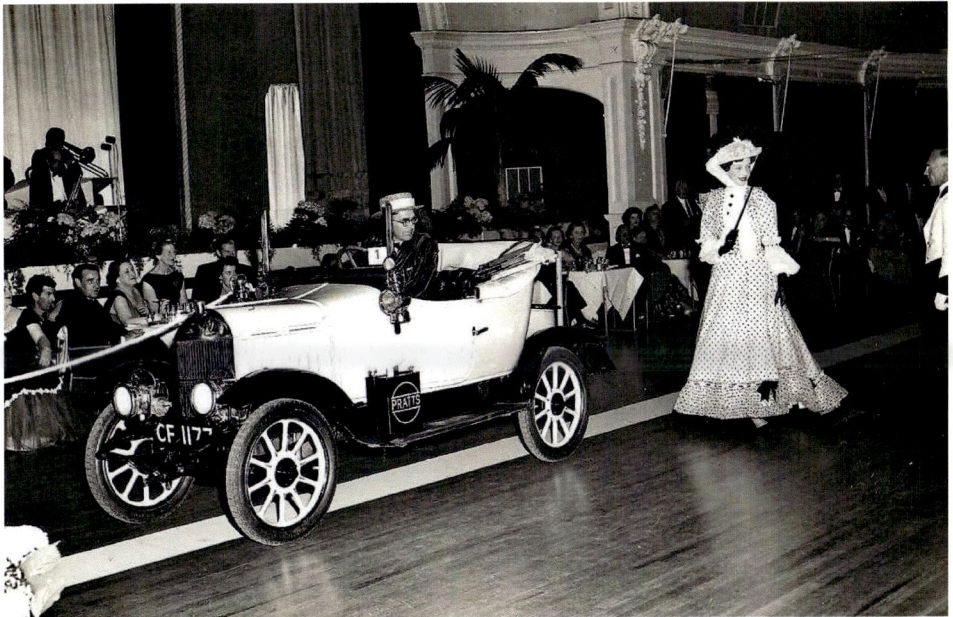

The Concours D'Elegance at the Winter Garden.

that Pietro was most proud of was his illuminated car mascots. One was in the shape of Pegasus (the winged horse) being held by Mercury with winged heels and carrying a bright torch. This sold for 12 guineas (about £700 in today's money). His most memorable design, however, was based on Eastbourne's own lighthouse. This stood at about 6 inches high and was made of bronze coated with nickel silver. Adverts show that it acted as a 'tell-tale for the rear light' and also as a thermometer to register the heat of the engine. The lamp could be fitted with either a green or a mauve aspect. The mascot retailed for just £3 (about £150 today). Adverts for these Eastbourne-made car accessories appeared across the country including Scotland. The *Eastbourne Gazette* of March 1931 reports that the Eastbourne Lighthouse mascot was 'known to motorists around the world' and, in fact, when the famous pilot Amy Johnson visited Eastbourne in August 1930 Pietro presented her with her very own 'Beachy Head Car Mascot'.

Motoring has moved on from the 1930s but one local company has adapted with the times: William Morris Caffyn, who started to stock motor fuel in 1871. He was bought out by his sons, who went on to establish a successful motor business which now has dealerships across the south of England and a turnover of millions. Their headquarters is still in Meads Road, and if you want to see some early motor cars that once graced the streets of Eastbourne they have several on display there.

The Concours D'Elegance continues in Eastbourne in the form of 'Magnificent Motors', an annual free motor show held on the Western Lawns. There is a splendid selection of vintage and classic cars and motorcycles which attracts over 25,000 people every year.

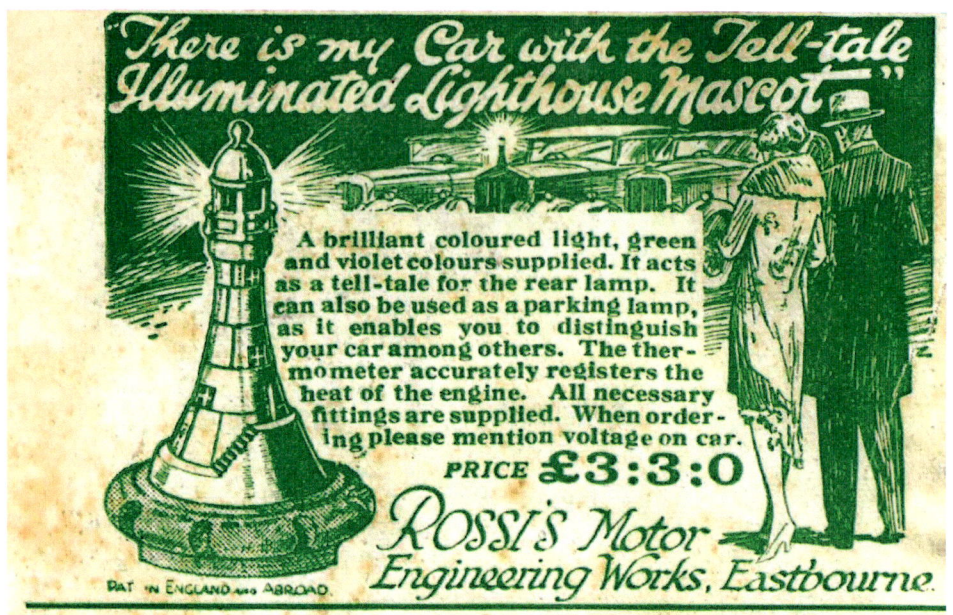

Above: Rossi's Lighthouse car mascot.

Below: Magnificent Motors on the Western Lawns. (Eastbourne Borough Council)

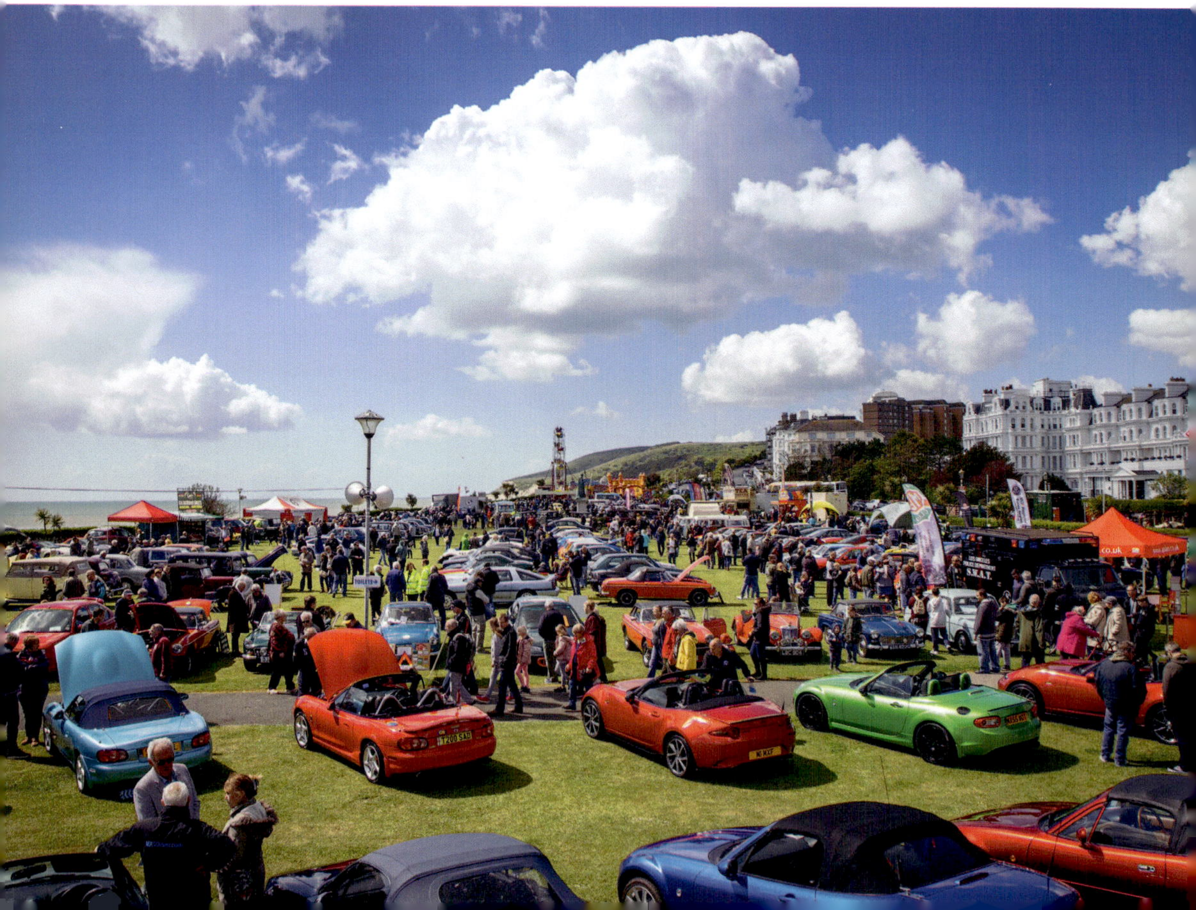

Notable Visitors

One of the earliest 'tourists' to Eastbourne was John Taylor (1580–1653) who visited Eastbourne just before he died. He was previously a waterman on the Thames and is remembered as 'The Water Poet'. He wrote 'I was on my female beast borne to a feast borne at a town called "Eastbourne".' Unfortunately John tells us virtually nothing of the town but he enjoyed the food and drink. He was particularly impressed with a 'a high and mighty drink called Rug'. He wrote 'Was never such a rare infused confection to provoke sleep and stupefy the senses – No cold can ever pierce the flesh or skin of him who is well lined with rug within.'

It has been suggested that 'rug' was a strong beer possibly mixed with blackberry wine. And what to eat with a glass or two of rug? A small local delicacy called the 'wheatear'. This tiny bird was found in great numbers on the Downs and thousands were caught each year by shepherds who set up traps for them. They would be cooked and eaten whole, bones and all, or sometimes put into a pie. John tells us that they taste like marrow and 'lusciously dissolve in the mouth'. Their name was thought to be derived because they nested in wheat but this is not true – their distinctive plumage means 'wheatear' is a corruption of 'white-arse'.

One of the most famed entertainers in the Victorian era was Charles Stratton, also known as 'General Tom Thumb'. Just off Seaside are some single-storey houses known as 'Tom Thumb Cottages'. But surely they were never the home of the famous 'dwarf'?

In August 1865 the following advert appeared in the *Eastbourne Gazette*:

GENERAL TOM THUMB
His LITTLE WIFE and their INFANT DAUGHTER
Will give their CELEBRATED ENTERTAINMENT
at the WORKMANS HALL.
The public are respectfully informed that this is the
LAST APPEARANCE of the General in public.
NB: At the 11 o'clock performance they will appear
In their Wedding Costume.

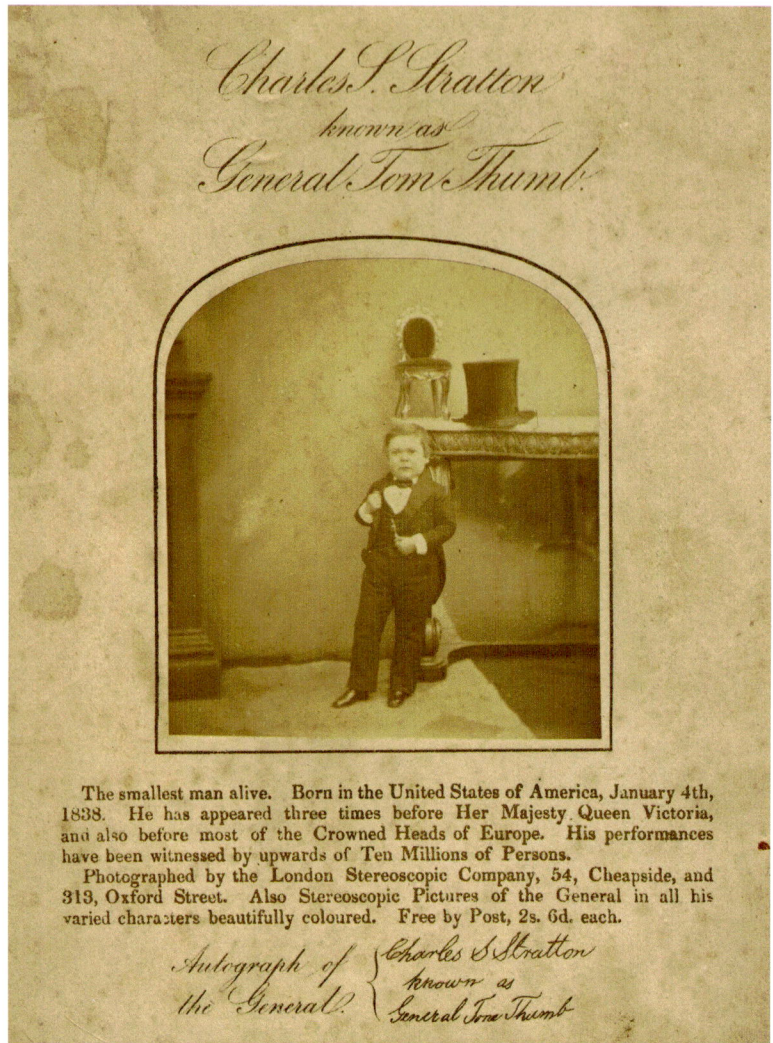

A souvenir of Tom Thumb's visit to Eastbourne.

The Workman's Hall is now known as the Leaf Hall and is just a few feet from 'Tom Thumb Cottages'. Sadly though he did not stay there – they were far too small for such a famous performer who had toured the world and appeared on more than one occasion before Queen Victoria herself. No, he stayed at the much posher Sussex Hotel.

Eastbourne was known for its good selection of private schools and several famous people were educated in the town. They include:

George Robert Sims (1847–1922) attended a school for young gentlemen in Grove Road. He was a journalist noted for his work amongst the poor of the East End of London. He was fascinated by crime and particularly the Whitechapel murders and indeed is still believed by some to be a suspect for Jack the Ripper. George wrote poems (his most famous being 'Christmas Day at the Workhouse')

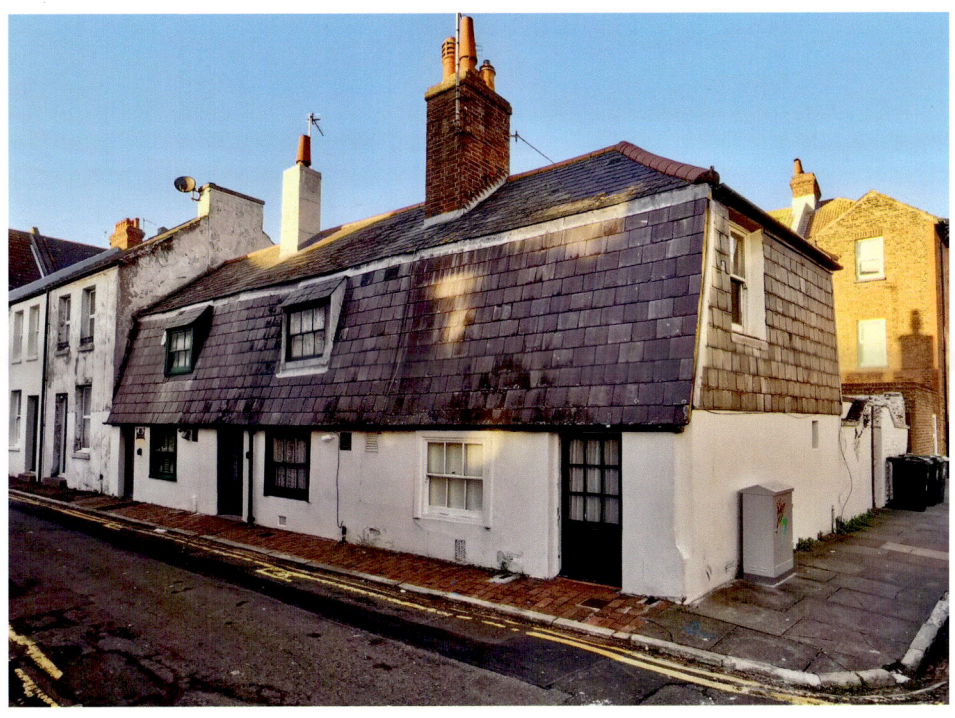

Above: Tom Thumb Cottages.

Right: George Robert Sims.

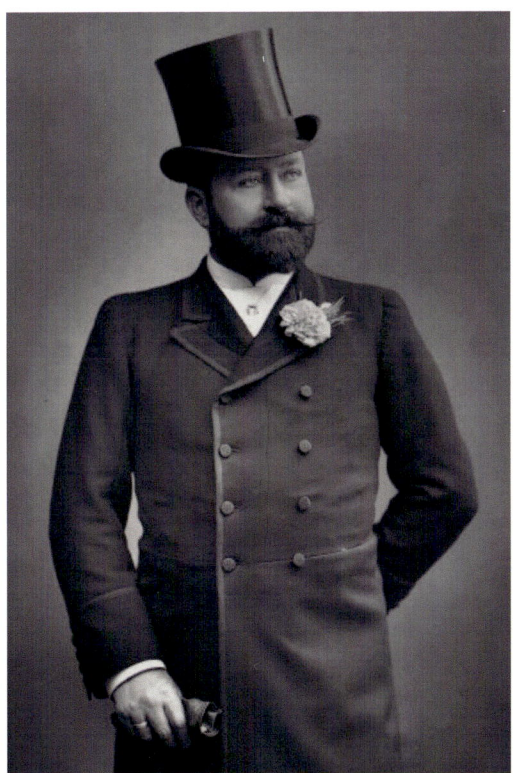

and many plays and novels under the pseudonym Dagonet. He wrote crime stories featuring Dorcas Dene, one of the very first fictional female detectives.

Scientist Frederick Soddy (1877–1956) was born at No. 6 Bolton Road and was educated at Eastbourne College. He worked with the New Zealand physicist Ernest Rutherford with the relatively new science of radioactivity. He coined the word 'isotope' and was awarded the Nobel Prize for Chemistry in 1921. Soddy was clearly a man ahead of his time. In 1904, whilst at Cambridge University he made an extraordinary claim saying that the atom – the smallest particle of matter could be turned into a weapon that could destroy the earth. He also studied economics and in the 1930s suggested that energy should not be obtained from exhaustible stocks of fossil fuels.

Edward Morgan Forster (1879–1970) is better known as E. M. Forster. He attended Kent House School in Staveley Road. He was a prolific author and was nominated for the Nobel Prize for Literature on no fewer than seventeen occasions. Today he is remembered for his novels *Room with a View*, *Howards End* and *A Passage to India*, which have all been made into successful films.

Eric Blair (George Orwell) (1903–50) attended St Cyprians School (locally known as 'Kippers') between 1911 and 1916. Blair was later a journalist for the *Observer* and also a war correspondent for the BBC. His novels *1984* and *Animal*

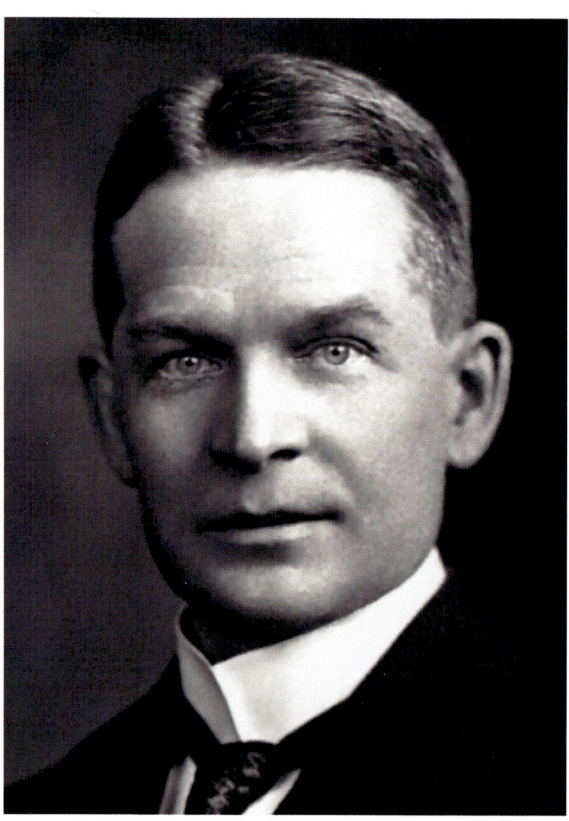

Frederick Soddy.

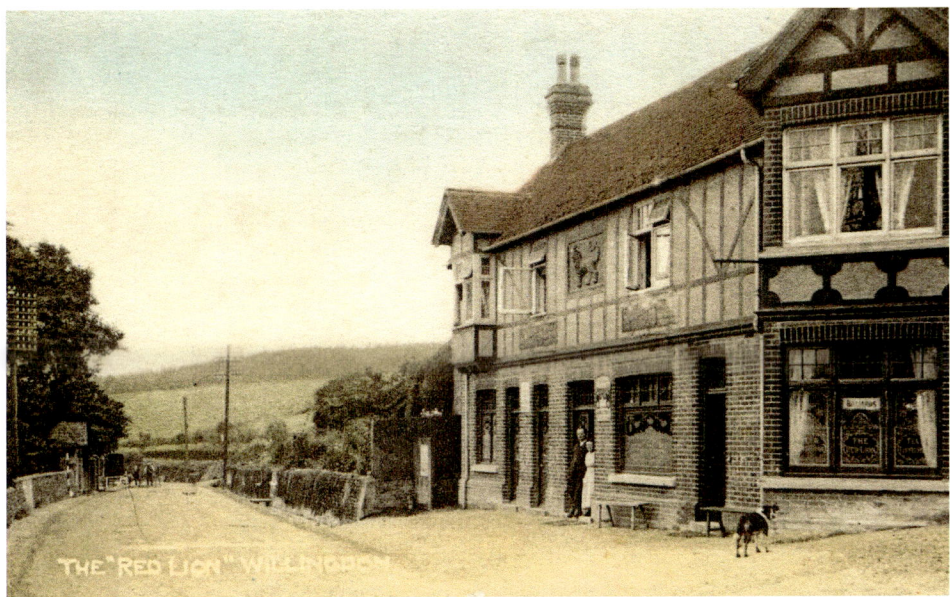

Above: The Red Lion at Willingdon
where Farmer Brown got drunk.

Right: Cecil Beaton.

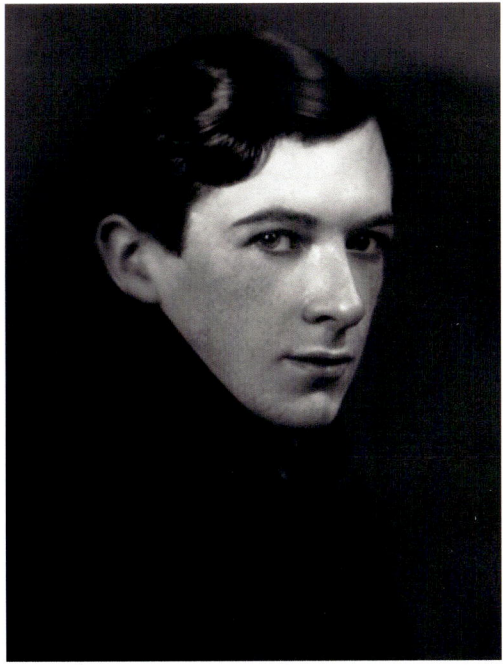

Farm are probably best known, the latter being set in Willingdon where, in the
first chapter, Farmer Brown gets drunk at the Red Lion pub.

The photographer and designer Cecil Beaton (1904–80) also went to 'Kippers'
School. Beaton became a photographer for *Vanity Fair* and *Vogue* magazines.
He worked as a war photographer during the Second World War and took many

official photographs for the royal family. He is remembered for his set designs for the 1964 film *My Fair Lady,* for which he received an Oscar for Best Design. Beaton had affairs with several glamorous men and women including Greta Garbo and Adele Astaire, the sister of the dancer Fred. By the way Adele went on to marry Victor, the son of the 9th Duke of Devonshire and an Eastbourne street (Astaire Avenue) is named after her.

Gavin Maxwell (1914–69) went to school in Eastbourne and is remembered as a naturalist and author, his most famous book being *Ring of Bright Water,* which was later made into a film.

The famous air-ace Sir Douglas Bader (1910–82) was educated at Temple Grove School in Eastbourne. Despite losing both legs when he crashed a plane in 1931 Bader joined the RAF and fought in the Battle of Britain. Notwithstanding his disability he was promoted to Wing-Commander and was stationed in Sussex. He crashed in France in August 1941 and was taken prisoner by the Germans, being held at the infamous Colditz Castle. His life was celebrated in the 1956 film *Reach for the Sky* and he was an advisor for the 1969 film *Battle of Britain,* the opening shots of which were filmed over Beachy Head and Eastbourne.

Notable Residents

Dolly Shepherd and the First Mid-air Rescue

Few people who met Dolly Sedgewick, an WRVS Volunteer at their former HQ in Hyde Road, would have suspected that this sprightly pensioner had such an adventurous life.

Dolly was born Elizabeth Shepherd in Potters Bar in Hertfordshire and in 1902, at the age of sixteen, worked as a waitress at Alexandra Palace. Here she overheard

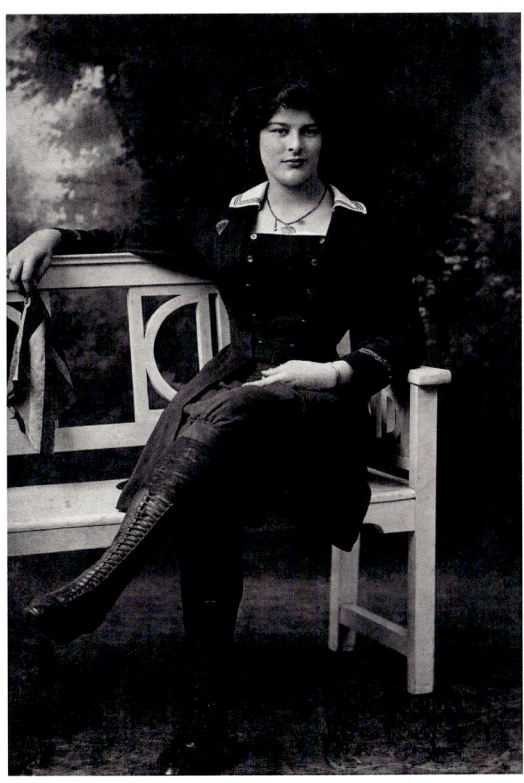

Dolly Shepherd.

a conversation about the American Wild-West Showman Samuel Cody, who was performing that evening. She volunteered to help in his act, which resulted in a blindfolded Cody shooting an egg off her head.

Cody was an early pioneer of balloon flight and this was probably why young Dolly became interested in ballooning. However, not for her to ascend gently skywards in a basket; no, she was suspended from a trapeze underneath! Following just thirty minutes of training, she was soon jumping from balloons with a parachute and appearing at events and fêtes across England and Wales. This was clearly a dangerous occupation – on one occasion in 1905 her balloon malfunctioned and climbed to over 15,000 feet. She had another narrow escape from death in June 1908 when at 11,000 feet she jumped from a balloon with another female parachutist. Her colleague's parachute became entangled with the balloon and failed to open, so she grabbed onto Dolly and the two fell to the ground at great speed, but survived. For this Dolly was credited in performing the first mid-air rescue. Despite spinal injuries she said that the accident would not dampen her ardour for skydiving and by September she was performing jumps again. Strangely on several occasions she also visited and descended into coal mines, saying that she wanted to go as deep into the earth as possible as well as high as possible.

In spring 1912 she was alone in a balloon when she heard an ethereal voice saying 'Don't come up again or you will be killed'. She took the hint and never took to the skies again – well not for a while. During the First World War Dolly worked as motor mechanic in France and in 1919 she married. Dolly moved to Eastbourne in 1962 and became an active volunteer at the WRVS. At the age of ninety she returned to the air again and flew with the Red Arrows. Her daughter Molly also lived in Eastbourne and followed in her mother's footsteps when she made a parachute jump at the age of sixty-seven!

A Keay Eastbourne Family

Henry William Keay was a remarkable Eastbourne politician having served as the mayor of the town no fewer than seven times. He was a magistrate and an active member of Eastbourne Council for over fifty-three years having sat at the very first council meeting in 1883. In 1922 he was presented with the Freedom of the Town.

Henry was born in Brighton in 1848 and as a teenager worked at the W. H. Smith bookstall at Brighton railway station. In 1868, at the age of twenty, he was transferred to Eastbourne to become the manager of the railway station bookstall. Four years later he established his own bookshop in Terminus Road.

This was so successful that in 1905 he was able to sell his business to his former employers, W. H. Smith. As a distinguished bookseller, he became the president of the Associated Booksellers of England and Ireland. He held this position for twenty-six years, during which time he standardised book sales across the country making it fairer for authors, publishers, printers and sellers.

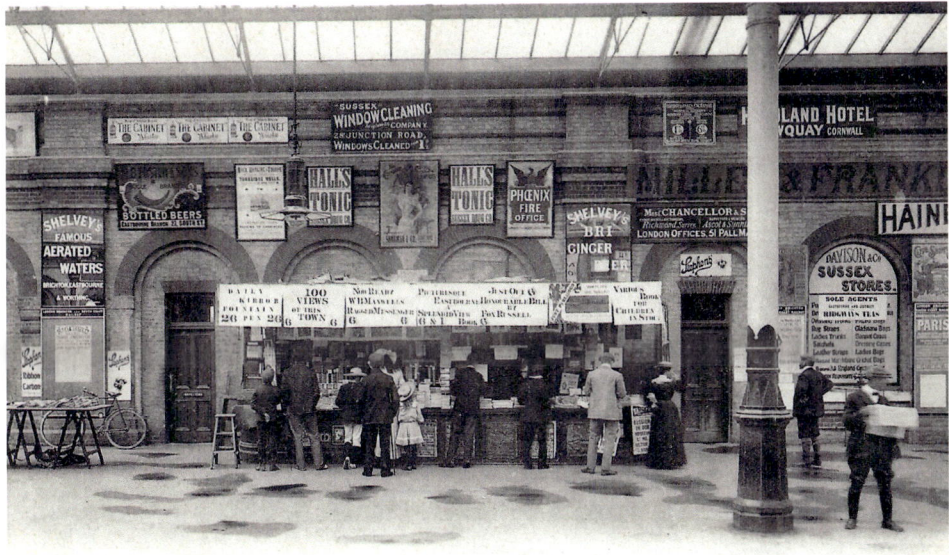

57 EASTBOURNE. — Intérior of the Railway Station. — LL.

Above: The bookstall at Eastbourne station.

Right: Henry Keay.

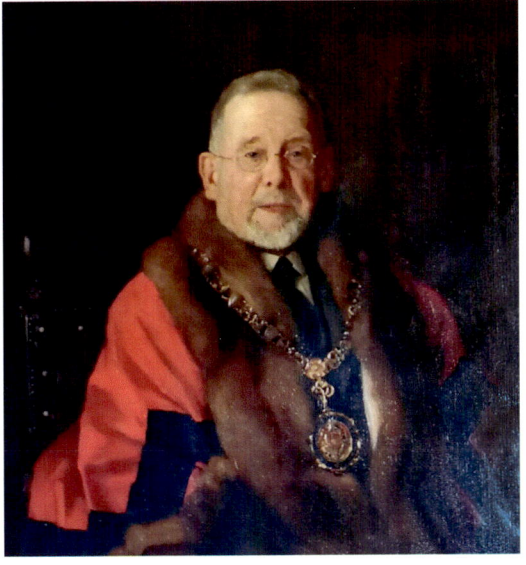

Henry's passions were music and drainage! He was instrumental in establishing Eastbourne's municipal band and orchestra and for many years ensured that the town had a reputation as a venue for first-class music. He realised that if the growing town was to maintain its position as a clean, healthy resort, it had to have good drainage.

Henry inaugurated the annual Hospital Parade to raise money to support local hospitals and was President of the Eastbourne Chamber of Commerce. On his death, the mayor, Alderman Wheeler, said that Henry was 'in every sense a perfect

English gentleman' and was the 'Father of Eastbourne Council'. The *Eastbourne Gazette* said: 'He was the last of the Great Eastbournians and one of the creators of the Eastbourne that we know and love today.'

Henry married in 1875 and made his home at No. 1 Clarence Villa, Enys Road, and later Elmsmeade in Meads Road. He had three sons, each worthy of note.

Wilfred Keay was born in 1888. He was a lieutenant in the Kings Own Yorkshire Light Infantry when he was killed in action at the Somme in 1916. His name appears on the Eastbourne War Memorial panels at the Town Hall.

Ethelbert Keay was born in 1877 and was a borough surveyor for Eastbourne Council. During the Second Word War he volunteered to be a fire warden. This was a dangerous job as Eastbourne was one of the most heavily bombed towns on the south coast. On the morning of Saturday 3 April 1943, Eastbourne was busy with shoppers when the warning sirens blared across the town. Ethelbert helped to shepherd shoppers into an air-raid shelter in Spencer Road at the corner of South Street, near St Saviour's Church. The shelter was a rectangular building with 9-inch thick brick walls and a 9-inch concrete roof. Sadly the shelter received a direct hit and everyone in it, including Ethelbert, was killed. His name is now inscribed on the Eastbourne Civilian War Memorial at the Wish Tower.

The Civilian War Memorial at the Wish Tower.

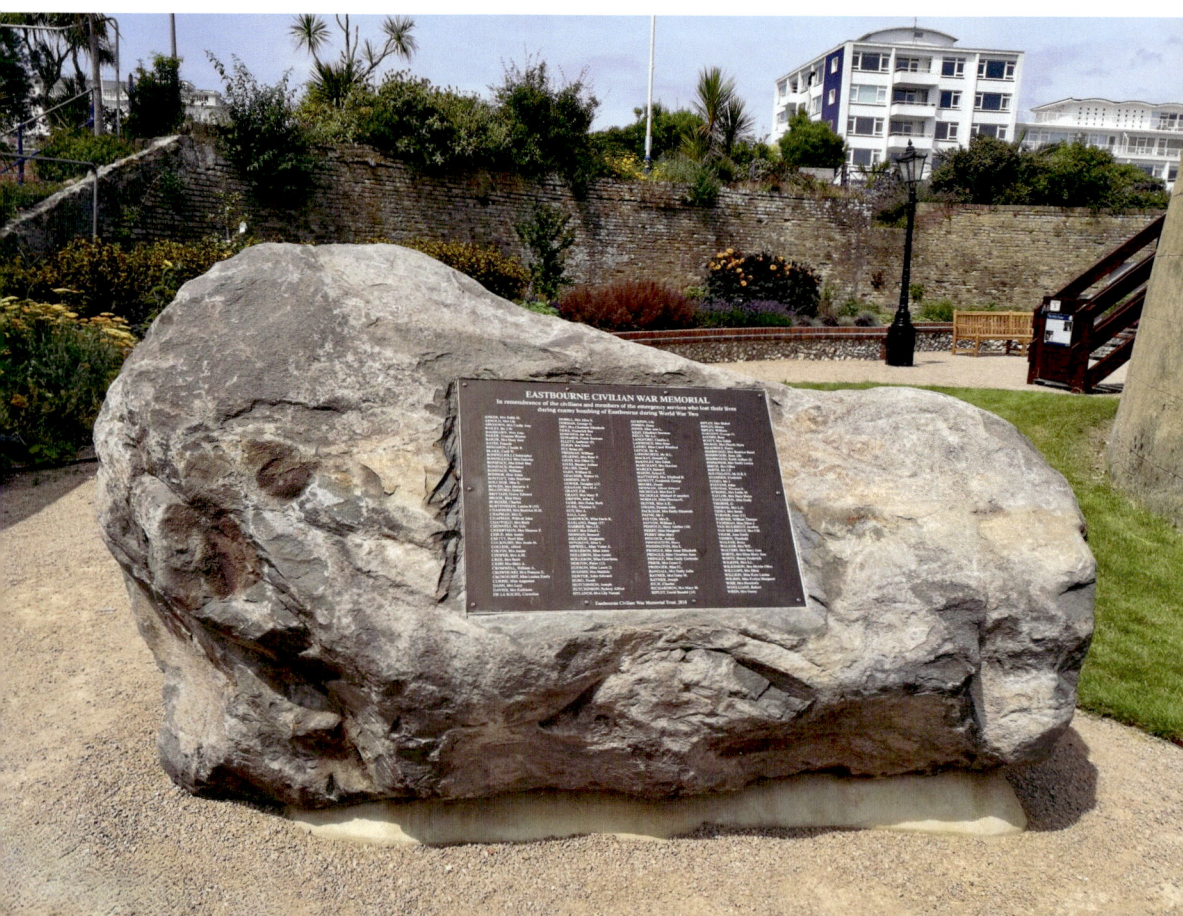

Lancelot Herman Keay was born in 1883. He was educated at Eastbourne College and later at Brighton School of Art. His first appointment as an architect was at Norwich City Council where he was later promoted to Head of Architectural Services and was responsible for the restoration of the Guildhall. During the First World War he served in the Royal Engineers but whilst in France in 1916 he received a gunshot wound to the back and was evacuated home. He recovered and later saw service in Egypt. On return to civilian life in 1921 he was appointed Chief Architectural Assistant to the City of Birmingham where he was responsible for designing and building 16,000 new homes.

In 1925 Lancelot was appointed Chief Architectural Assistant for the City of Liverpool and in 1929 became the 'Director of Housing'. He wanted people to live in healthy modern houses and was responsible for slum clearance and four massive development schemes to provide social housing. These estates became models for similar housing schemes around the world. One of the council houses that he designed was No. 20 Forthlin Road, Liverpool, the childhood home of Paul McCartney and according to the National Trust that now owns it, the house was 'The Birthplace of the Beatles'.

Lancelot was the President of RIBA (Royal Institute of British Architects) from 1946 to 1948 and served on the post-war National Housing Advisory Committee. In 1947 he was knighted. The great architect was also a sports fan (apparently he wrote to ITV on several occasions about their wrestling programmes) and in 1956 he sponsored eight benches to be placed at The Saffrons, Eastbourne's central sports ground.

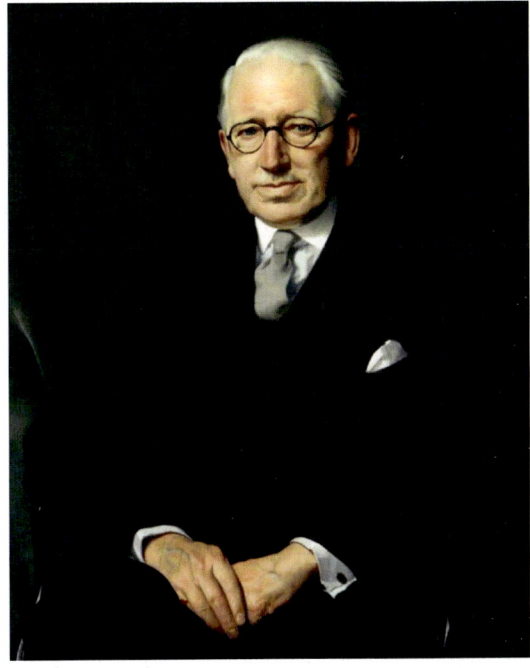

Lancelot Keay.

Ellis Kelsey – A Phenomenal Photographer

The Kelsey family moved to Eastbourne around 1893. Joseph had been a successful tailor in Richmond Surrey where he supplied the Royal Household's staff with livery. His wife Martha and their two adult children, Ellis and Edith, moved to a large purpose-built house in Upper Avenue, Eastbourne, overlooking the railway coal sidings. Ellis was a music teacher and the house had a huge music room with a massive church organ and two pianos. He was an associate of both the Royal Academy of Music and the Royal College of Organists and for some time was the organist at St Mary's Parish Church in Old Town. His main passion, however, was photography.

Ellis probably bought his first equipment, a half-plate mahogany and brass camera with tripod, at the age of twenty-four in 1890. This would have cost between £20 and £30 – about the annual wage of an average worker in those days. The expenditure on his hobby would have been considerable as, on top of the camera equipment, he would have needed apparatus to develop and print his photographs.

Ellis took thousands of photographs; to start with family portraits and pictures of his home, garden and pet cat 'Bobs', but he soon became more experimental and more artistic. He particularly enjoyed taking photographs under difficult conditions such as in the rain or at night. Many of his photographs can be considered as works of art and in 1899, one of his photographs was accepted for an exhibition by the Royal Photographic Society. This was the first of nearly a hundred photographs he exhibited at photographic exhibitions across the country over the next fifteen years.

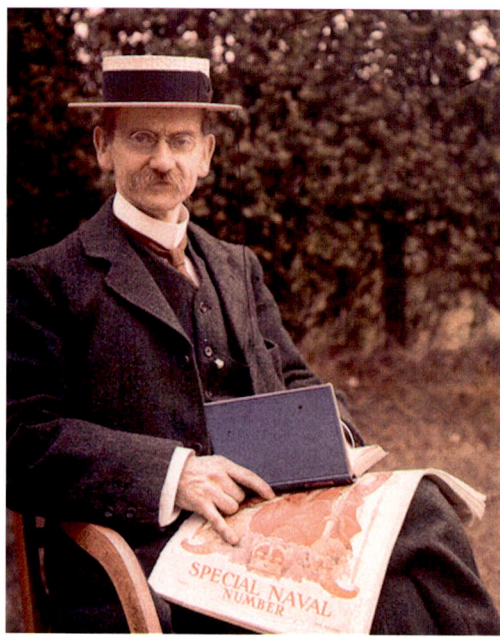

Ellis Kelsey.

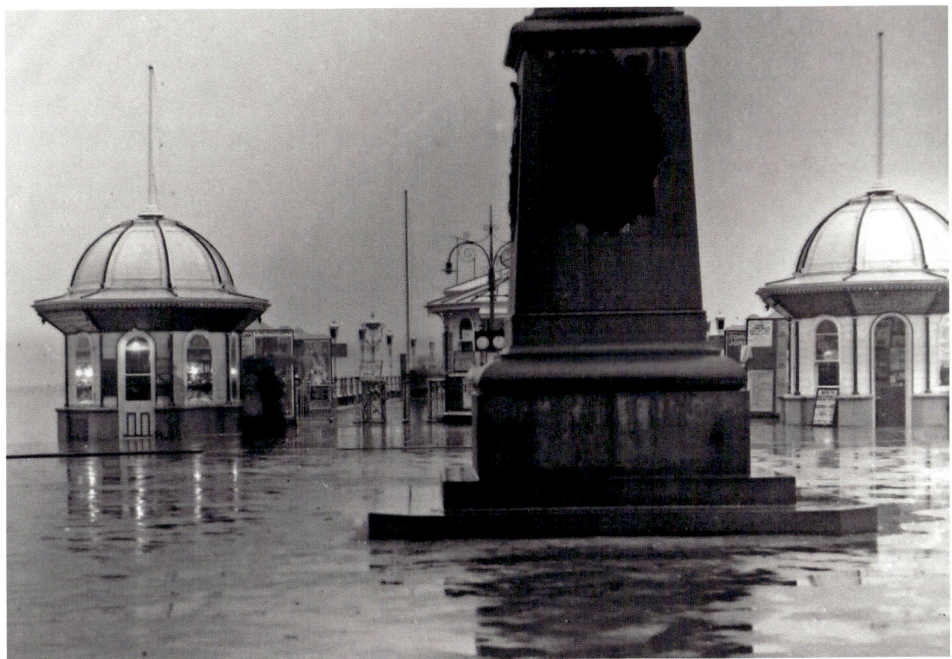

The pier in the rain.

In January 1899 Ellis gave a slide show to the Eastbourne Photographic Society at the Town Hall. His subject was 'Eastbourne by Night' and the *Eastbourne Chronical* reported that his photographs surpassed expectation. When he exhibited in Leicester, the local press said that he was one of the finest lantern-slide makers in the country and his photographic effects were staggering.

The Eastbourne Photographic Society met regularly and, as well as displaying his photographs, Ellis would also provide a musical accompaniment. One of the society's committee members was Mr J. C. Wright, a local councillor and historian. He was friends with my great-grandfather Ebenezer, whose daughter, Bessie (my grandmother), was herself a talented photographer and was later the secretary of the 'Eastbourne Box-Brownie Club'. I like to think that she met Ellis or at least attended some of his lectures.

Ellis enjoyed travelling by train and photographing engines, although in 1901 when the council proposed working with the London, Brighton & South Coast Railway to build a large engine works in the town he wrote a letter of protest to the local newspaper complaining that 'The presence of a great number of workmen on the seafront every weekend would not be desirable and visitors would not welcome such additions onto the already busy parades. I hope that all Eastbournians who take pride in their beautiful town will protest against such a desecration.' The engine works were not built.

In 1914 Kelsey started to use the Paget Process to produce colour photographs and I believe this photograph of Meads Road was one of the very first colour

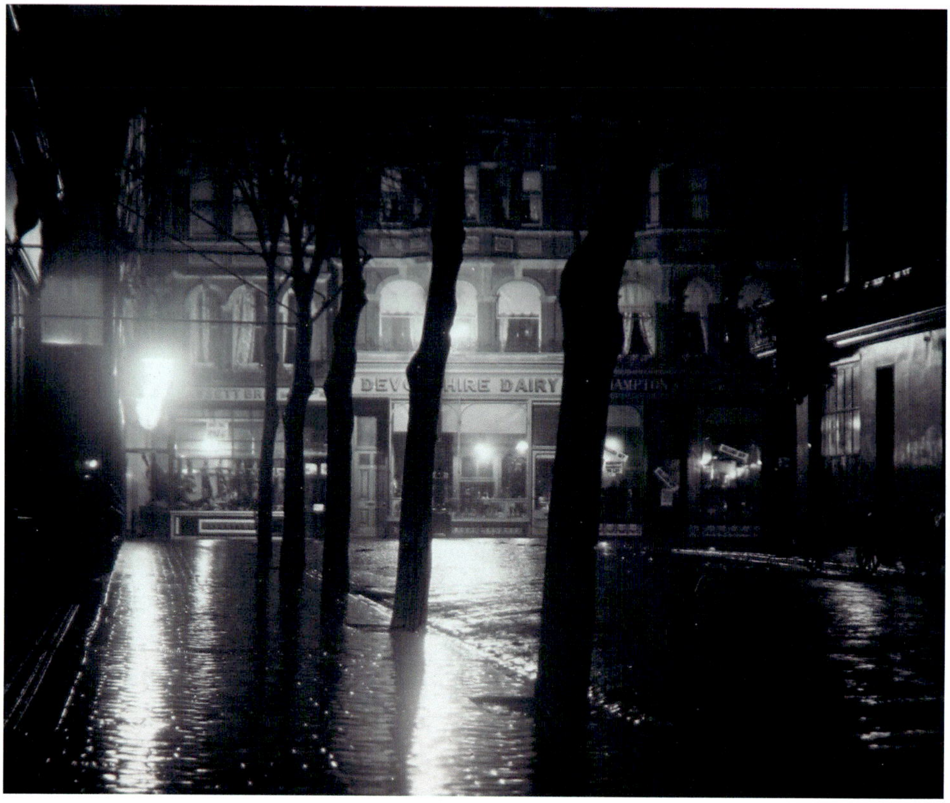

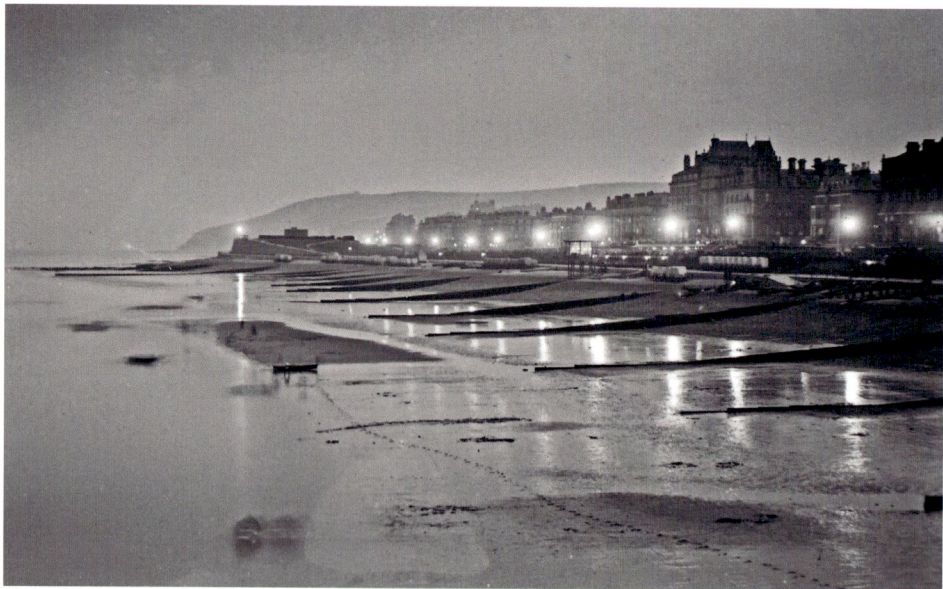

Kelsey's picture of Seaside Road junction of Susans Road.

The seafront at twilight.

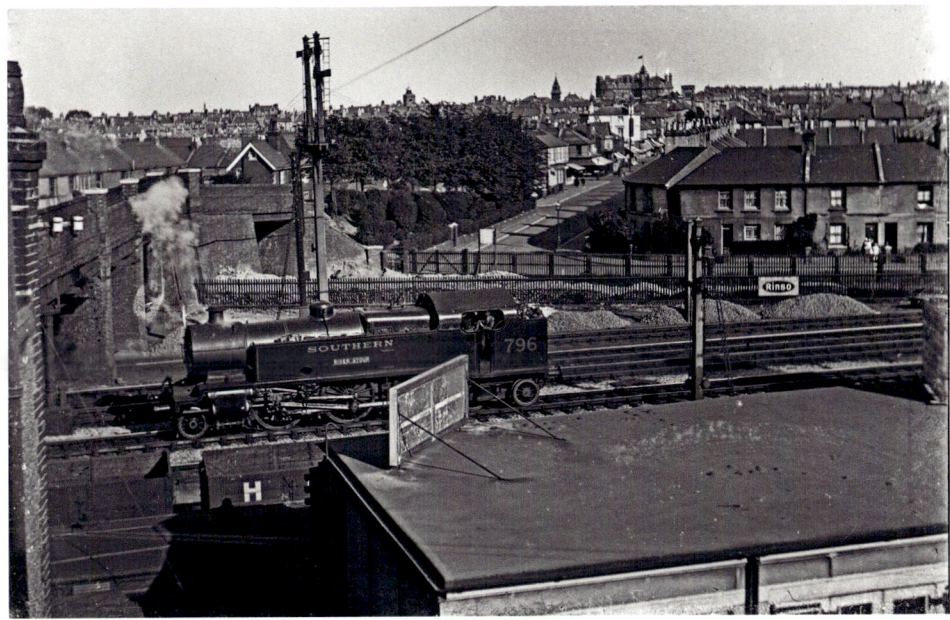

Kelsey's photo of Cavendish Railway Bridge.

photographs taken in the town. His spectacular photographs give us an insight into Edwardian Eastbourne.

Ellis married in 1931 at the age of sixty-four and moved to Seaford with his wife and sister. He died eight years later and is buried at Seaford Cemetery.

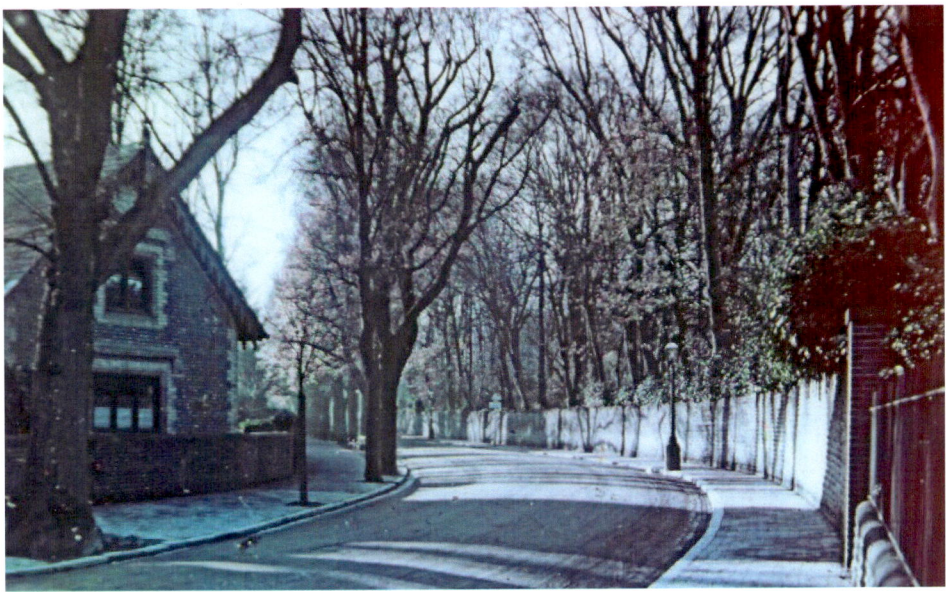

Meads Road.

Conclusion

I started this book with mention of my great-grandfather Ebenezer Roberts and I would like to end with him as he was quite a character. He was born in 1867 in Old Town just a few yards away from where I live today. At the age of thirteen he was working as the driver of a goat chaise (see page 55) but in his early twenties became a greengrocer in Church Street. He married Bessie Bennett of Lewes in the North Street Chapel (later Cavendish Place Chapel and now the Eastbourne Greek Orthodox Church) in 1897 and I was interested to read that the ceremony was at 8 a.m. Ebenezer was a strict Baptist and sometimes preached at the Grove Road Baptist Church. He was certainly anti-Catholic and this is evidenced by the speeches he gave as the head of the St Mary's Bonfire Society.

My great-grandfather became a builder, decorator and thatcher. He was responsible for thatching the clubhouse of the Redoubt Bowling Club and the nearby telephone box.

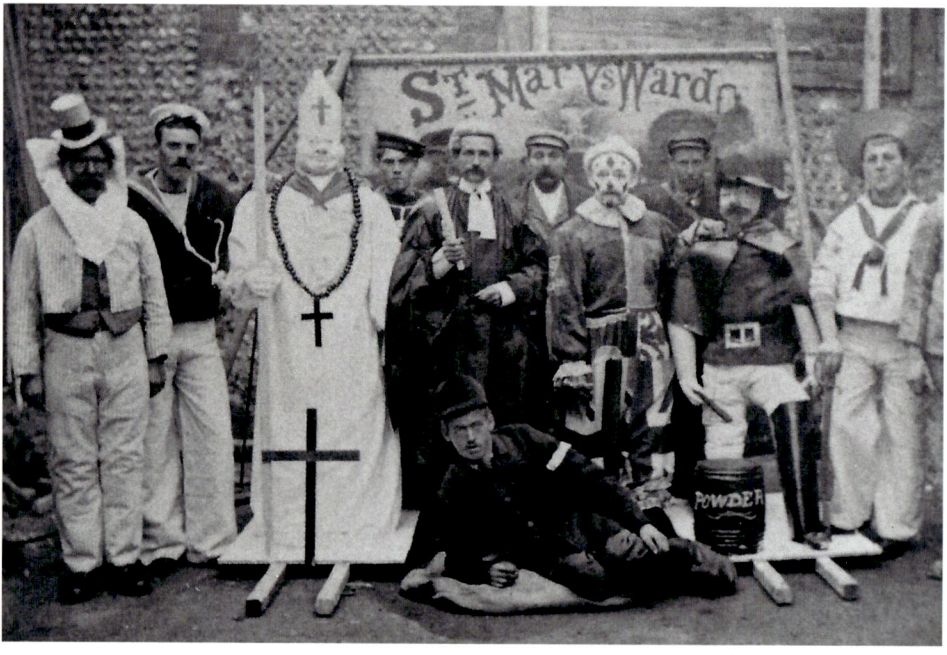

My great-grandfather (centre) holding one of his bonfire speeches.

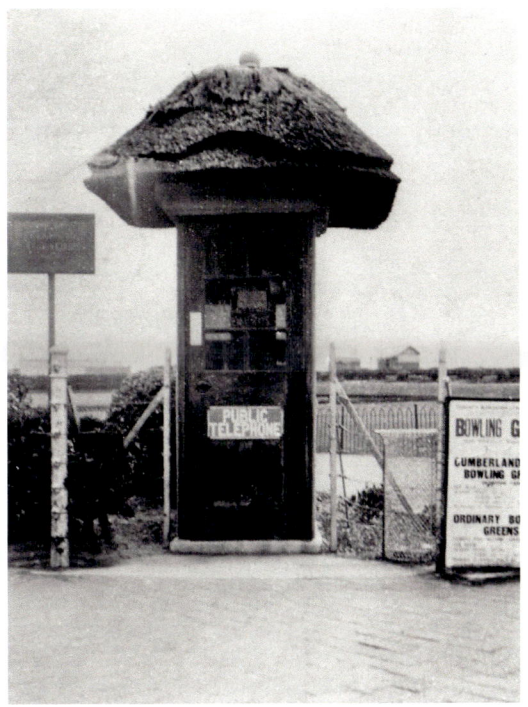

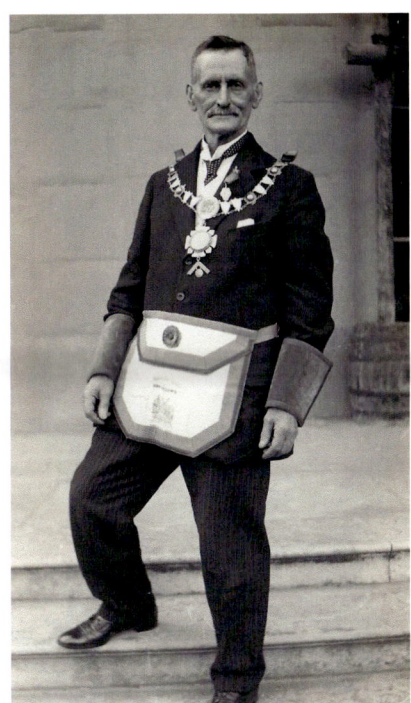

Above left: Eastbourne's thatched telephone box.

Above right: Ebenezer in his Oddfellows regalia.

In his later years he was the chairman of the Eastbourne Old Age Pensioners Committee and a 'sick-visitor' for the Eastbourne branch of the Manchester Unity of Oddfellows. In 1933 he became the Lewes Provincial Grandmaster for the society.

As you have seen from the first paragraph of this book, he also wrote poetry. In 1898 he wrote a poem about Queen Victoria becoming England's longest serving monarch. He had the poem printed onto a card and sent it to Buckingham Palace and was thrilled to receive a response. He would go on to write many 'royal' poems. which he would post to Buckingham Palace. His last royal poem (on the wedding of Princess Elizabeth and Philip Mountbatten) was published just a few days after his death in 1947. Ebenezer loved Eastbourne and I do too.

How You Can Celebrate Eastbourne

You can celebrate Eastbourne in many ways, by shopping and dining out locally or joining one of the dozens of local groups who strive to help Eastbourne and Eastbourne people.

The Eastbourne Society is concerned with the town's rich architectural heritage and the Eastbourne Local History Society researches and collates the towns long and fascinating story.

There are a large number of friends groups and there are many volunteering opportunities that you can support. The RNLI Museum, built in 1898, became the country's first lifeboat museum when it was reopened in 1937. Volunteers run the museum and shop and are always happy for new recruits.

The Friends of Eastbourne Seafront were established in 2022 initially to protect our iconic bandstand but now have expanded to protect the whole of the 4-mile seafront from the Sovereign Centre to Holywell. Volunteers dressed in blue jackets regularly patrol the parades assisting visitors and are particularly busy during the

Eastbourne Airbourne. (Eastbourne Borough Council)

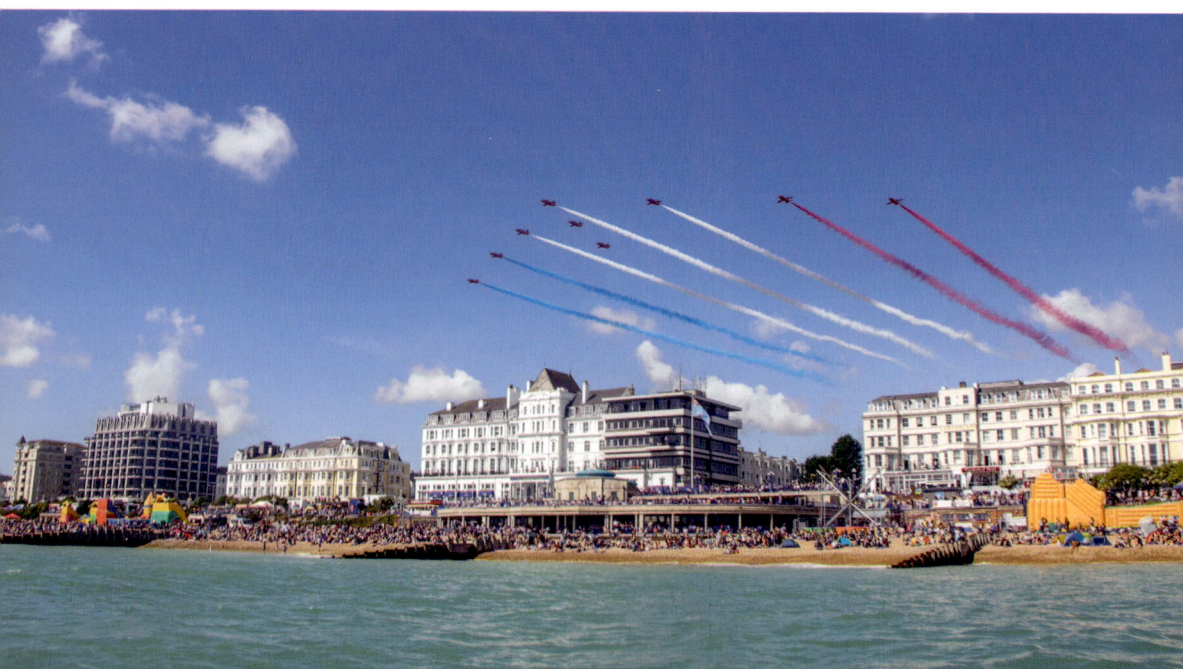

popular Eastbourne Airbourne air show, which attracts up to 750,000 people each year (and boosts the local economy by some £20 million).

There are several friends groups for our open spaces including Meads, Manor Gardens, Seaside Recreation Ground and Motcombe Gardens. These groups have regular clearing sessions as do the Friends of Ocklynge Cemetery, who have done splendid work in clearing graves of the famous and the forgotten.

The oldest of the Eastbourne friends groups is the Friends of Eastbourne Hospitals, which was established in 1948 as the Eastbourne Patients Association. In the last seventy years they have raised over £18 million for the hospital. In 2015 they raised money to buy a Da Vinci surgical robot.

Volunteers assist people at the Towner Art Gallery, which in 2023 was selected to host the internationally acclaimed Turner Prize. To complement the exhibition, contemporary art installations appeared all over the town.

Eastbourne has a rich, long pedigree. Many people will say that the town's heyday was in the Victorian period but it remains a super place in which to live or visit.

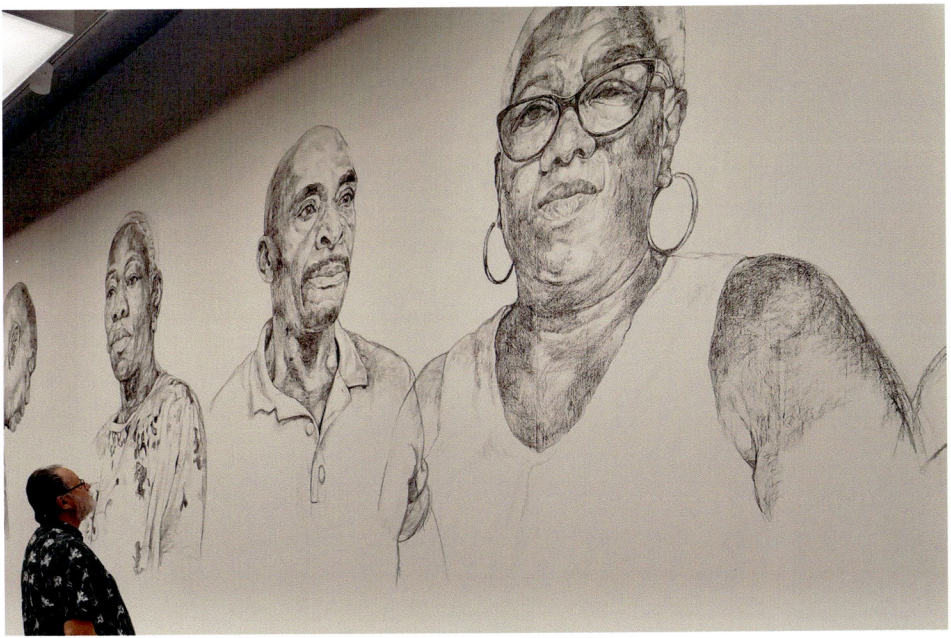

The author with a Turner Prize entry at the Towner Art Gallery.

Acknowledgements

I would like to thank my wife Mandy for her patience, as well as the following:

The Compton Croquet Club
Steve Holter
Bob Cookson, Kim Adams and Lionel Moth
Ben Franks of Seaford Museum & Heritage Society
Mick Hyams, Russell Owen and the late Nat Gonella, Eastbourne Local History
  Society
The Eastbourne Society
Eastbourne Library
Jack Brownall of Eastbourne Council
Kelly Van Doorn and Katherine Buckland of Heritage Eastbourne
Bill Burns and Simon Chiefetz of www.atlantic-cable.com

I have used a wide variety of resources for this book but particularly the following
books:

A Brief History of Eastbourne (Albert Enser, 1976)
Roller Skates and Rackets (Eastbourne Council, 1999)
The Playhouse on the Park (Edward Thomas, 2000)